WHISPERS FROM THE TREES

This book is written in an uncommon dialogue

as it contains messages straight from the Tree souls

and all care was taken to keep it

exactly like was delivered.

Thank-you for your patience with the book.

In our endeavour to get our messages through to everyone, we give so much and at times we give our lives to become timber, paper, or pulp as you call it, in order to produce materials, needed to make a description of things, but in this instance we are proud to be able to supply the product needed to make our words seen and read, so our messages of love, compassion, and wisdom are passed on to our human friends; so we can all live together peacefully. We bless those who take the time to read our words, it means the world to us.

Tree souls from this planet

WHISPERS FROM THE TREES

BOOK TWO

TALKING TO THE OLDER AND LARGER TREES

THE BOOK

GLENDA UNGERMANN

To order additional copies of this book, contact:
Xlibris
1-800-455-039
www.Xlibris.com.au
Orders@Xlibris.com.au
775277

Introduction

WHISPERS FROM THE TREES, book two or *the book* as the Trees call it, is a unique blend of love and beautiful messages from our beautiful larger and older trees that reside on this planet at the moment. I mentioned in Book one that I channel their stories which give us an insight into their lives, their loves, their passions, their spiritual beliefs and give us valuable information to guide us. They are happy to share their past lives to show us, we really are connected on a soul level, they show us how important they are on the planet and to us humans as well. I have built up a great deal of trust with them over the years and it is the trees who want their stories to go out to the world for all to see, hoping it will give everyone the chance to delight in their lives and understand their plight as well.

I believe this second book is more compelling with more information, and advise for us, proving they listen to us in our lives, and know more than we do at times, especially about the solar system we live in. They live in harmony here and have many things going on in their lives, we could never dream off.

All that is required from us is friendship, fellowship and understanding that we are all souls on our own, evolutionary journeys and believe that our souls are exactly like theirs, we are you and you are us. One day we will all understand this and live together completely in the circle of life.

The messages in this book are similar to our own spirit guide messages.

Yours truly,
Glenda Ungermann
The Trees Storyteller, a voice for the Trees.

Vanara

VANARA is a beautiful tree in a resort on the island off FIJI. I asked if she would like to speak to me during my visit here?

You are very welcome to speak to me tonite. I am filled with pleasure to be able to represent the trees on our island. I was planted here many moons ago to be able to grace this lovely island, with love and respect and to be of value to our planet.

I would like to talk about our planet and the many changes we have all under gone in the last few years, many changes and many guises to suit all our needs.

We live as one and that means we live for ourselves first, seeing to our needs and then we are able to pass on the knowledge that is needed to help grow our planet and solar systems.

Each one of us is, as important as the next one. We understand our place in this time space reality. Our planet MOTHER EARTH as she is known is vital to everyone who lives here at this given moment. Mostly we see the humans changing everything, but little do we know, everything that is changed, can be reverted back in an instant. Violent storms and large winds can sweep across the land and waterways and gravitate towards negative energy spots and destroy all in its wake.

This you have names for like hurricanes and cyclones and tsunami. These unstoppable forces are nature at its best, ridding the planet of excess negative energy. Churning the energy around and around until it gravitates it upwards and out, pulling all negative forces away, clearing the space to let only positive energy remain. Afterwards a feeling of calm and the breath of a new start imminently beating.

Our island sees these storms frequently, washing it clean. Leaving the energy to flow and nourish everyone in its wake. We see everyone banding closer together to survive and spreading more love than ever before. This is natures way of reuniting all souls back together often forgetting the very things that they did not agree upon beforehand.

We know our planet is beautiful and divine in so many ways but still the humans, change the waterways and build the roads that cost our lives, all to suit the living plans to congregate together. We don't understand why they all wish to live so close by each other, except for amenities I guess, running water etc.

I am a leader tree, one who helps others in a time of need. We council the young to build them strong so they too learn to be become leaders in this lifetime.

Do you have a past life you would like to share with us?

I believe I do, I was a slave in troubled times, bought and sold many times over to work and honour my master.

This was a troubled life, not one of pleasure. We originally were free to live our lives and war conquered our land and our lives. We were sold into slavery.

A primitive practise in any lifetime; some masters were strict and horrible, making us work the fields, daylight too dark. It served no purpose really except to degrade our lives of any value and hinder any personal growth.

Many years later we were sold to another master who valued our input and allowed some of our views and we were able to find love and build families of our own. A little grace but still a slave. We were much happier than ever before. I married a beautiful woman as none of us were young by this stage and we were given a gift, a child from our union.

This child was given his freedom as a young man. He built his life and educated himself, well. My wife and I stayed on in the plantation as payed employees, not ever knowing the outside world, and not game to venture out either. Taking some ones freedom away, inhibits their soul and their soul growth.

Thank-you for speaking with me it surely was a pleasure to meet you in person.

Much love VANARA

ROMANO *The Great tree spirit.*

ROMANO lives on the island of FIJI.

It truly was an honour to meet you and your friend in person.

We knew you were here, on the island and we knew it was your rest time.

We were truly respectful of your visit.

I was so excited that you came to me and I appreciated your time. I am known as a great tree spirit especially in this area.

We find real longevity harder to achieve here on the islands as we are constantly in the path of destructive storms, which cost our lives all too frequently.

I am excited to tell you of my life, as I am a pillar of strength to all who need help. The original native people of the islands understood us well and used our bark as medicines, and antidotes, and as time goes by; we see the new generations loosing the abilities to heal using our methods. We see inspiring religious cultures moving in and taking over time-honoured traditions. This is not easy for the people here to understand or accept, as they do not understand the need for change.

My name ROMANO comes from great circles or soul families from far away.

This name is a name of greatness and carries much responsibility.

I will receive accolades on my return home for the greatness of this life.

I will move on to a much higher calling the next time around.

I shall be returning to a life of time travelling through the universe to recommend lives on this planet EARTH, to be of great value for our soul lessons.

What seems like a simple life here, is full of information for our souls as we learn to relate to ourselves, and others in a way we are not able to do so, when in spirit. Here, we learn to work out every part of a problem (problem solving as you call it) it sounds so simple but at home, those lessons are glossed over and here we learn to work out each and every detail of the aspiration until we understand it perfectly.

That is the learning skill to add to our resume of life. So every time you have those little annoying problems instead of dreading them, welcome them into your life and you will learn to handle them a great deal easier.

Each time it will become so much easier, it will no longer be your lesson and you can move on to other, more important goals.

Drama does not require you to be insulted, just learn from the ordeal, and let it go. I think this a very good statement for all of us to learn from, as drama is draining on all of us, if we honour it, understand it and then let it go, our lives would be so much easier.

We love to talk about lessons here on the EARTH plane, as they pave the way for all of life's lessons to follow. Life is bountiful here everything you need is here at your finger tips just allowing the thought to exist, brings reality closer to you every time.

Set time aside every day to imagine the best life you could possibly live and go with the flow until you are living the dream that you want, it really is that easy.

We hope we have been of help to you to understand the flow of our universe and how it really works. Imagination is all you really need.

I send you love and best wishes. God speed to you and yours

Romano.

Glossary

I put a call out tonight to speak with any tree wanting to talk to me and GLOSSARY answered my call.

I am situated on the ISLE OF CAPRI.

I am eager to speak to you. I have many details to discuss and I feel I am able to help and add to the book, which will help our purpose as well as yours.

I am a leader tree of great value to our universe and able to assist others with all kinds of problems.

I am a top, ranking official in the area of soul growth. We help all of our young members to cope well in all the storms, that life hands out. We always choose to succeed no matter the calling. We council them until they are strong and self-supporting once again.

My name is GLOSSARY. It is a name to be very proud of representing my family back home. I have had lives in a variety of places on different planets in our zodiac of time. I am a time traveller that dwells on any plane to learn soul growth from a variety of lives.

At present I am a living tree on your beautiful planet here to experience the essence of this life and help as many others as I can. I am situated on the ISLE OF CAPRI.

I am hundreds of your years in age and have many years of love, left to give before I return to the fold, and then I will move on to a new existence, which will serve my next appointment.

We find it difficult at times to work with your words, as it is very limited to express our feelings. We feel and communicate much easier through our vibrations to each other, never having to find a word that defines what we wish to say.

We wish to appraise you as your language is difficult at best, but we are doing the best we can, to communicate our ideas to you to learn about soul requests and the journey beyond.

We choose to descend into these lives, to learn the value of gaining information for our own soul growth. We do this consistently in and out of lives, and at times we feel like we are playing parts in our own movies, always being the star attraction.

Our lives are always more important to us than any one else's.

When we experience the loss of another soul, close to us, we grieve for some time but then maintain equilibrium as we balance our lives once again. We are here for ourselves only, we cannot do for another, or we will lose ourselves fully and waste our time here and have to repeat the lesson once again.

Loving another is a valuable part of life, so too is learning to let go.

Once we understand the journey we are on, we realise we don't really lose them, they are acting out their lives in order to obtain their soul growth as well. We choose to do this together for the lesson to be of more importance.

I ask GLOSSARY, do you have a past life that you would like to share with us?

Yes I believe so, a life that I have experienced on another planet, and one of great importance.

I was born a male and raised into a life of importance to teach others the way forward. I now believe it was also a very valuable lesson for myself as well.

I was a legend in my own time. I was able to secure a large portion of land that otherwise would have been invaded and most importantly over run by dissidence who would have killed our people.

My team was able to hold it long enough until help arrived and the best outcome was achieved. On my arrival back I was heralded a hero and given a warm welcome by the Queen, who offered her daughters hand in marriage.

An offer, which was too good to pass up, so I spent quite some time getting to know Princess Persephone herself. We were warm and wonderful together and built a lovely foundation on which to base our marriage on. One year later we wed.

I was appointed a royal Prince and given a bodyguard, my loyal friend JOSEPH.

Together JOSEPH and I led the army in many battles across our lands and fulfilled our duties.

My wife and I raised four strong sons, one of whom was a future King. We were from a planet called LORDS, a planet still in existence to this very day.

My name was PRINCE HARRIETT DE COSTELLO.

I thank you for allowing me to share my story, it means the world to me. Many thanks, love from

Glossary.

AUGUSTINE. 1400 years old

I now wish to start the life story of one of the most significant trees on this planet.

His name is AUGUSTINE. This tree still resides to this very day in CHINA.

AUGUSTINE is fourteen hundred years old and remembers everything in detail of his life and times. He remembers the times of great wealth, and also times of poverty, and depravation of the liberties of the culture of that era. It was called the Sui dynasty era.

AUGUSTINE is a very large tree that attracts many visitors daily.

My story starts as a small seed blown by the wind to germinate in the soil, not far from my mother tree. Life was very favourable for me, I was granted everything, I ever needed to grow. I grew and I grew, enjoying my position and always knowing my family trees were near by, living and breathing the love they needed to continue in their lives. As time passed my family and I became very large trees, enormous, compared to other hill top trees.

We are enjoying a network of vibrations, which we use to communicate with each other. We still use this to this very day. It is our way to teach love and inspire each other every given day.

Little by little, our beautiful family was starting to disappear over the next hundreds of years that followed and as the human population increased. This was a slow process, but painful to watch. We are capable of living many of your centuries in one lifetime. I feel I am at the peak of my life right now.

This particular tree seemed more important to me than most others. I am not sure why but he has my undivided attention, and a love for him that feels grand. He was bought into my world quite differently than the others. I had an article in the TOWNSVILLE DAILY PAPER about communicating with the trees and I received a phone call from a TOWNSVILLE resident who, just came back from CHINA, her name was KERRY. We met and enjoyed a coffee as she told me her story. She had just visited this tree as part of her holiday there. She had photos and told me she could feel he was so sad. She said I had a compulsion to visit him it seemed, nothing could stop me from going to him as their were set backs along the way. She pressed on like it was something she had to do. How this story unfolds later took both of our breaths away.

We live with the ability to seek many things, the past, the present, and the future in all its glory, the past with all its valour. We remember the past lives, past loves, and Past loyalties.

Past Lives for me have been many, judicial lives of religion, barbaric lives of survival, sweet lives of love and family. Love is the sweetest thing, but as it plays out, lies and betrayal play out as well. This is the one I recall foremost in my memory.

This was a life as a trader in the Far East when, exotic spices and dried foods and furs were traded for gold. Gold was usually in cups, coins, and vases in those days.

We sailed the high seas to deliver goods, it was a very enchanting life. A life of heroism and survival for the fittest all rolled into one. To survive was to succeed. I lived half way through this life and died to an accidental happening.

A life as a sailor in those days was wine, women, and song. A life well lived and still treasured to this very day.

Past Loves feels so sacred, so nurture them, for it gives the most blessed feeling of all. Perhaps I will get to finish it, one day my love and I. I feel it still awaits me and I look forward to that, finishing our very special love story.

Past Loyalties are the time we spend on this planet to show us all how we behave, how we learn, and how we have come here to play out our lives and learn to share in it, be as one. Love each other no matter creed or race.

As trees we live by this code. All of us are important, each and every one of us is equal in our eyes.

We need not of each other, for we exist happily by ourselves.

We enjoy each day for the joy it brings and the breeze that blows and honour us, our great lessons.

I have witnessed much fighting and bloodshed, much weather turbulences, right here around me at different times.

People fight instead of showing emotions. They find forgiveness too hard to achieve.

There is too much of this is mine and that is yours.

Time will tell, and everyone will realise, nothing belongs to him or her, but they belong to it.

As we live each day, our life plays out just as it should, it is all going to a perfect plan.

Each day is the perfect plan for us, no matter how the day plays out, it is exactly what you need to learn, to grow to achieve your life's purpose.

Past Experiences

Our past experiences are one that portrays life's difficulties or challenges.

We experience these to grow and to learn and to understand all of life's challenges given that at the exact time or timing isn't always filled with passion, as some lessons hurt us or allow us to feel great emotions, all at once.

Love, devotion, guilt, and jealously, anxiety and loneliness are great teachers.

Some lessons aren't always practical at the time however, great learning evolves from these, all to honour thy self.

Life is a learning curve each and every day, whether we realise it or not.

It lasts from the day you arrive here, until the last day itself.

It is all about the journey in between.

The present.

The present is the now time. It's the today of our world. I can feel the vibrations of the people who visit me, they're vibrations of speech and emotions. I can feel when love and fear is present.

Some love me as they are in awe of my many branches. My branches are like family.

They feel this as they to have many branches in their lives, their mothers and fathers, their brothers and sisters, their sons and daughters.

Others who visit have fear in their hearts; their own emotional fears in their lives and also fear for me, hoping I will survive their culture and trails. Many just hope they leave me alone to grow naturally by myself as I have done for generations so far.

The future

We feel the future in all it's finest vibration, so much more to come, to help us achieve all that we came here to do. We look forward to that.

We receive accolades on our return home, for the joy we bring, and the love we give.

We have compassion to help us understand this wonderful MOTHER EARTH who gives us all life on this planet.

I honour you our great EARTH MOTHER.

Do you understand the past history of your land?

Only suffice to say, it was a period of great struggle. Leadership battles over who owned the most land, the most possessions and who had the most power over the people. It was not a great period in history to be proud of, when high power reined or so they thought, even through the struggle, people rallied to not loose themselves completely, even though by day, they behaved a certain way, while at night they regained their own beliefs to be strong in their own opinions. That was nice to witness so they did not lose themselves completely.

I asked AUGUSTINE, can you tell me about your life growing up during the ages?

Well yes, as a young tree growing up I was a taller tree than most, I had what you would call a very good head start. One never knows how ones life will pan out, you just live every day enjoying life, and always making the best out of every minute, this is how life should be.

I asked AUGUSTINE, Our lives seem different, we seem to be trapped into a cycle of supporting ourselves, gathering money to survive to feed our families?

Trapped is right. Well! Who did it, you did it to yourselves or more precisely generations of your people started this, slightly different system called bartering.

Previous to this people lived in groups like most native tribes do, water was used for all. Food and clothing was shared and everyone raised the young to ensure survival was paramount for all. Time will tell, one day the humans will learn, no one exactly owns anything, not the people, or the land. Until then it will be a hard lesson for all. One day we will all be one.

Enlightenment

Enlightenment is to seek your true self, to leave behind all that you have been taught; to learn anew and too now, follow your heart and see what lies ahead. Teach others too, not to be afraid and to learn what is in their heart and soul.

Find the passion, live the dream, and find your very own purpose, the one thing you came here to achieve.

Hold your head up high, and be who you really are, with no regrets.

This is the code we live by.

Love, Loyalty, Honour, Wisdom, Compassion.

Love and Loyalty is for-most for your self, than for any one else. Honour is very important, being honourable to your self first and then showing honour for all.

Wisdom is to be wise, to think it out for yourself and then decide to share it with others.

Compassion is to have patience with yourself while you grow, learning not to be hard on yourself, to love yourself first. Then learn to pass it on.

Using all of the above, we learn to sail through our life living and breathing and trusting our lives will be sacred as well.

We spread our seeds far and wide in the hope a new seed germinates and grows into a marvellous tree, which loves life to the max. That is the cycle of life.

This will be ever lasting, till the end of time.

I asked AUGUSTINE about the culture of the country over the past years? And he said. This has been a hard life for many as poverty, power, religion, and greed took over.

Power and greed go together, poverty encases religion at times.

People have suffered generations after generations, all to learn the power of greed.

Greed is ugly, poison in fact, it benefits no one in the end.

Religion also has a gift, some find themselves, while others are persecuted in the name of it. It goes both ways. Only the lucky ones survive to recall the lesson.

But generation after generation is playing out the lesson, now the young wish to choose for themselves, but the conditioning is strong.

Each lifetime is making headway. There is much more choice available than ever before. This will take a lot more time to work out but eventually they will get there.

I asked the question of tourism?

Tourism is changing the face of our country. They wish to show the positive now and leave the old traditions in the days of the bygone era.

I am also a tourist piece, where people from all over the world come to gather to look or to learn, or just marvel at my magnificence. Rarely do they ever actually speak to me. One doesn't know it's possible, I suppose.

I see them, each and every one of them. I can feel and hear their thoughts, some care while others, do not really understand. I can feel their pain and enjoy their passion, and smile for the photographs, that pleases me. I care not for the visits but I love it when they care. It shows they also care for themselves and that's a splendid thing. Life improves every given day I believe.

I asked AUGUSTINE about survival?

Our system is complex, it is a bit like how your body works, your body knows how to extract minerals and vitamins from your food to sustain your bones and skin tissue, it works the same really.

As I grew, my root system anchored itself to the earth, where it finds the nutrients and minerals to sustain my growth. I also draw the moisture I need to survive.

I am capable of storing enough moisture to see me through a dry period until rain falls again.

The Earth also accommodates us well. It has underground river systems, large and small, sometimes very tiny veins that can deliver enough moisture to keep us going. We feel and know exactly when the rain will come and know how to monitor moisture until then.

In the last few years, the quickening has began, Quickening is a term used to describe a time of great change for our universe which affects our planet on a daily basis. The times for rainfall have also changed. It could be days, weeks, and months different to the usual time. We understand the climate changes and respect the process. These changes will settle shortly and begin again in the year you call 2025. Cosmic order has to be achieved to align this planet in orbit, so life as we know it can continue.

I expect to still be here to celebrate your Thirtieth Century. I predict for most of you, there will be many more lives in and out of this galaxy, some may even get to call by again, and how thrilling that will be for me. I recognise the souls that have been here before, even if they do not.

Some of my very special friends like KERRY recognise a calling to me without understanding why. I see them for the souls they are and not their disguises this lifetime. I feel them when they arrive and I watch them and seek them out.

It consoles me to see a true friend indeed, on a pathway going about their lives, just the same as myself.

I must say GLENDA I am enjoying communicating with you and one day I will tell you where you fit in, in the cycle of my life. Until then take care my good friend.

I have to admit this scared me a little, I was not sure what to make of it and with present duties of looking after my parents in their final years, I left Augustine's story for the next twenty-two months.

The day finally came and I was ready, I picked up his photograph and called him, I said I am ready to know now. He said Are you sure and I said yes, and today I spent some time with Kerry. He answered, I know her well, she was saddened by what she saw, when she visited me.

She felt and understood my pain, pain with no retrieval I thought, but my prayer was answered. Love always finds a way. She and I were kin a long time ago, another time, and another place. I was looking for an answer and this beautiful lady helped me even though she didn't understand it at the time, but she never forgot me and as she returned home and saw an article in the newspaper about the tree whisperer and knew she had to meet you. And here we all are, friends forever now and writing words on my behalf in the book, which will help the humans, understand us better.

I am so grateful for that.

I have a message for KERRY.

Be still my sweet, for again we will travel, for now know the favour you bestowed on me will never be forgotten. Finding your path is like finding new love. It often arrives right before your eyes and is joyous in total.

Blessings, to you my dearest friend KERRY.

I understood this as a part of her journey this lifetime to find him again, a soul finding a soul mate.

Beautiful, beautiful, AUGUSTINE dare I ask? What is the connection between us two?

I am glad you asked, I have waited for you to be ready with that question.

We were twin souls born to the same parents at the same time in heaven.

It is not often that the creator officiates these requests, but our parents deserved the privilege. A child is a divine offering from the creator. To be given two at the same time is quite a unique gift.

We spent our young lives with our beautiful parents until we became of age. That was quite some time ago. We are what most would call old souls now.

We came from a time of privilege, to be most honoured and we have done our lives, requiring us to learn to grow our souls and to now give freely to a cause.

My cause is to be a tree of greatness, one that resides here for a long period of time.

And yours GLENDA, is to try to get humanity to understand the life of a tree, is of equal importance as the human life itself.

This will be a long battle and it won't finish before your lifetime here is over, however you do get a point across to benefit the trees and mankind to change their thinking and except each other as equal souls.

This will honour you with the accolades on returning home to complete a charge.

A charge, which will take you to the next highest level of completion to a master.

This will be your crowning glory. A job well done and you will move on to your next project.

We are kin, actually twins born in heaven at the same time, a rare treat for many.

We will work together many times over in the future, until we decide to rest our limbs and stay home. Then we will have earned the respect of being an elder.

And KERRY is the all time love of my life. We will venture many more lives together and find the love we lost many lifetimes ago. We have forever to accomplish these dreams, there is no hurry, finding her this lifetime meant I found you as well, which is a great treat, and it inspires me to complete my goal.

This is what I meant when I said I would never forget the favour she bestowed on me, that it would never be forgotten. All my love to you girls, I now have the connection I have so longed for in this life, to go on more happily than ever before.

Sending light and Love to you both, every given day.

I know I was blown away, and so was KERRY, we were speechless we sat there with our hands over our mouths going - Oh my God!

Then we needed another coffee.

AUGUSTINE, KERRY and I have decided a little later on that we will come and visit you, when the universe provides, we will be there. We would not miss it for the world, it is very important for me to be able to see you in person, that will give me something to look forward too.

Today AUGUSTINE would like to talk about truth and how important it is in your life. Being truthful is too only speak, what is in your heart and to not the make up a version that might sound better for someone else to hear. Sometimes the truth will assert its wishes upon you, but that is much better than to be untrue and hurtful, and be an unlawful version of what you imagine someone else wants to hear.

When you speak your truth there is no mistake in what you say, no shame in your eyes and your heart feels free. You have done your best, where as when you fabricate an untruth it just keeps going, leading into more uncharted waters getting larger each time, still speaking just to cover it up, it never ends and you fool no- one.

It just isn't worth it in the end.

When you speak your truth, it is precise, clean, and its over in one go.

After a while it is just easier to speak from your heart, say what you need to say and respect will be yours.

We don't bother with the interlude it's just to time consuming, so we speak from our heart every time and never have to look back and life flows forward in an instant.

This, you will find is much easier to forecast and build a better life for yourself.

Imagination. This is stardom at its best. We have worlds going on in our imagination that surpasses any life here. In this beautiful place we are free and uninhibited.

It is our own very special place where no one else is invited. In this place we write the stories of our lives, we pretend, we reinvent ourselves and we only please ourselves, no one else matters. This is where we feel we can be a child forever.

Quiet often books are written from our imagination where stories start and movies are made to entertain us from the ideas that are born.

Here is where we are most at home in this life. The outside world can be harsh and we feel at ease as our imagination never lets us down, it has chapters of high volume interludes on every subject available, to last our whole life long. These can be drawn from past lives and anything in between. We really come here with a wealth of untapped knowledge knowing everything is possible.

Inventions, ideas all come from somewhere, deep down at times, mostly you say it just came to me out of the blue.

We came here to do certain things at specific times in our lives, we don't always remember exactly what that is, knowing full well, we will accomplish it in our own time. It is our imagination that kick starts this process, ideas will start to flow giving you the taste of what will become, and then you finish the process easily.

As you grew older you were taught to shelve your imagination and ideas as being childish, something that sticks with you and you loose your drive to activate your imagination. For those of you who are headstrong, you never lost it because you knew it was yours and no one could take that away from you. Besides it is in your head and can only be yours, yours to drool on, play with and pretend and create all you like and so you do.

For some it has made them famous writing books, making movies, creating tools, and building homes, inventing great pieces of art as the list goes on. All these ideas come from somewhere, sometime or another and now get to live on in this dream you call life. Your imagination is the best tool you bought with you for this life.

Your imagination reminds you to love again when the time is right.

It reminds you every day life is worth living, because that is what you came here to do, so do it the best you can each and every day.

And then he added; I have much to say.

Intuition.

Intuition is that feeling of knowing, deep down in your core. The feeling you are given is always right. Your body follows the alignment, feels the energy of it, and knows it is a correct feeling. We watch as the humans second guess it, play with it, and convince yourselves that, it can't be right, and change your answer to that which, you would like it to be and within a short time it becomes apparent to you, that something does not sit right, it is not right and the feeling you were given in the first instance was truly correct.

This is the learning curve for all of us, we need to pay attention to what we feel in the beginning, however it is not as easy as it looks and we all struggle with following our intuition correctly. This is something that takes our whole life at times to understand and trust completely. When you master it, your life moves more peacefully and you get to enjoy every given moment.

Earths forecast

In my opinion, I believe Earth is a strong planet. She will be around for a long while yet.

We are all here to play out our lives and we do that well. We have also changed the way this planet was. The humans changed the rivers by damming them, changed the direction in some cases where they flow, and trashed the waterways with rubbish and steel. Sunken ships were left in the oceans to rot. Driven piles into the river beds so we can now drive over the rivers and oceans, dug out the riverbeds so we can now drive under the rivers in tunnels. It never stops and there's the land, well we could be here writing for years.

You have not left much untouched really. It was not your purpose to change the EARTH, but greed denotes it. The humans have been very selfish in their ideas and then, this is what we see, they make you all pay for it. It takes years but they happily take a little extra each time until all their requirements are paid for.

The planet EARTH is a strong being, she takes her place in the solar system and has requirements to adhere to as well. This, most humans call climate change.

It really is a solar change as she finds her new place in the solar system, so EARTH can stay on for many light years to come, this is the comic order she needs to follow, or she will burn up if left in the old position. This portrays out to changing weather patterns here on Earth. It is only a small discomfort in the scheme of things really.

After the humans have finished with planet EARTH we will still stay on to rebuild the area and reclaim the devastation left behind, all building material will in time break down. Then the planet will be given back to the tree kingdom to rebuild and revegetate. We have great tools to rebuild, we have love.

Love

I would like to talk about Love.

Love is a many splendid thing, as your song says and indeed it is, but what I would like to say is the love you feel for someone when you first meet them is handsome and grand.

Indeed you say, I have never felt this way before and you really cannot remember either, that is true and here is the BUT!

You really have because for every one you meet, you already know their soul from your soul pod. This is the place from whence you came and you predestined these meetings. Now there are other things in the mix.

Like karma, it plays a huge role. On your first meeting, you know whether or not you like someone or can't abide him or her. I am sure everyone agrees to that, that's your intuition kicking in, for some they become an acquaintance, a friend, or a foe.

Some relationships develop further into friendships that become love in a grand way and this usually leads to a partnership of a lifetime. This can be a truly beautiful soul, you can enjoy spending your time with, and sometimes for the rest of your life.

You really are amazing souls, putting all these things in the mix so that you get to meet as many delightful people, all sorts of animals and the beautiful trees that grace this planet, your whole life long.

Soul purpose

Our whole soul purpose here is to learn the lessons we put before ourselves each life.

Each and every one of us often say to ourselves, this is just too hard.

We wish to seek an improvement in our lives each lifetime and we know how strong we really are. Sometimes we have to push through the barriers to make a difference. Life is always worth the struggle and then you see the great rewards. As your life picks up you can focus on better things to come and they will keep coming as long as you stay positive, calm and relaxed and trust the universe does provide. All you have to do is flow along in the positive manor or frame.

We know we really are powerful beings in a limited world. We chose this time, to do our lesson here, so let's rejoice and pat ourselves on the back on a job well done. We will be very pleased with ourselves on our return home, because all we ever needed to learn was Love, in every form, in every way.

Love is foremost the most important lesson here.

The Book

We are very proud of *the book* that writes the stories of our lives. This has been a long time coming. The world waits with bated breath for this is the glue that seals us all together. There will be some who will not be interested at all and there will be others who will love our words and wait for the opportunity to read them all.

This will make perfect sense to those who love us. This will be the first time we have ever been able to tell the stories that make up our lives. Our stories have never been printed before.

We rejoice in being able to share our names, they mean so much to us. They are our mark of honour. There are so many of us who wait for a chance to tell our stories.

We understand it's probably not possible for all of us to get the chance, but we will do our best to share the opportunity with our peers.

I for one am very grateful to be able to tell my life and times. I am especially close to our friend GLENDA as we are like brothers or sisters as you call them. We are unique souls that started our journey together.

We have wonderful parents who wait for us each time we descend here.

They rejoice when we return home. Life is eternal. We do not ever die, as the Earthlings here believe. We just change form and go on our way, sometimes we take a break and enjoy the family unit that have been waiting for us to return.

It is unbelievable the love that awaits us. We also have a twin flame, a soul mate that is made to compliment each other. We fit perfectly and the love is uniquely ours. Music erupts in our ears when our twin flame is near, calling us together. This is truly a magical moment in our lives.

Death (as you call it) is an amazing experience. One should never fear the art of leaving the life here, it is a special event that unites us all immediately and returns us back to the positive energy that we are really made off. We are strong powerful beings of light.

This book will help the humans to understand our souls are all the same.

We are you and you are us. We say this time after time and soon enough you will understand the full meaning.

I am reverently calm and quiet and thankful for the joy *the book* brings to us. We need to be heard and only those who seek this information will benefit from our words. Please believe us when we say we love you all, because we are you and you are us, one cannot be without the other. My love and best wishes always.

Augustine.

Charlton

CHARLTON wishes to make connection with us now, he is an extremely large tree in NEW ORLEANS.

Hello! I am so excited to be able to speak with you and to be able to write my story in *the book*. This is the book that will change the perception of many generations; of humans for many years to come.

We have waited for this chance, not knowing actually how this was going to happen, just that it would. I am excited to be the one who helps this cause. It is a great opportunity for us to join forces and unite ourselves in love.

My story or my life started out simply like most others, except I am one of a chosen few who wish to stay a little longer to finish a great calling, one that will reside in my memory or my hall of fame for the rest of my life.

I chose to live here for at least until the turn of the next century and beyond. This is a positive calling for most of us who stay the extra distance to finish a charge in heaven. Many accolades are given to complete this successfully.

I wish to achieve my charge this lifetime. I am among many who wish to achieve this longevity, however sometimes it doesn't work out that way for all of us. Some die prematurely and others are removed by the humans for silly reasons such as something else needs to be in that exact spot, a heartless choice made by people with no respect for life.

I am indeed a lucky one, still alive and left in piece to live my life to the fullest.

I am a leader tree but I am so much more, I now lead the leader trees to be of help to all who need me and I embrace and love the job I have chosen to fulfil this lifetime.

I wish to tell you about my life, starting out like most small trees learning to survive all by our selves, is a challenge. Once we are large enough to survive, we then start on the agreement we wish to honour this lifetime. For myself it would be a pleasure to lead others into the new transition here on EARTH. This will change the way we think and do things for many life times ahead.

We are an energy source to this planet and the energy is changing every day, growing stronger and denser to provide a greater strength for this planet to survive.

We all have things to do and so does this planet, if she wishes to stay in the solar system. She is always working on realignment and growing to suit the new worlds.

NEW ORLEANS is a very time honoured place to reside in, now new times are mixing with old traditions. It is changing and leaving the old behind and creating a new blend of life. Gone are the wars, the slavery, and old ideas that are now changing the shape of this nation.

We see drugs being a major problem in to days lives. We fail to understand why one harms one self. Everyday one needs to centre the love on one self and place you in the most important position. You are the only one that counts, as you cannot do this for any other, only the self. Therefore you are the most important person in the world.

Bringing harm to your self simply does not make sense. This is usually a cry for help to say that you are not coping with life. A cry that usually goes unnoticed by many.

In our world we reach out to each other to send love and healing and be the source of guidance to our brothers, but in your world it goes back to monetary gain.

No one helps unless you can pay for it and those in need generally can't find any money, so they go unnoticed and sometimes they don't complete their journeys. These are our choices this lifetime, sometimes we can't make it with out help. We are proud to say for ourselves help is always offered and accepted in most cases.

We know the love on this planet is increasing every day and we are so thankful of that. This trend will increase hundreds of fold yet, until we have a large majority all understanding, mainly of themselves and where they fit into the universe. Then the universe will unfold and allow the world to see every detail in accordance of the universal laws.

How we live right now is important, we are all working through our own learning process. Each one of us is reeling from feelings and situations that are either attached to karmic lessons or other lessons we bought forward with us to achieve.

All lessons achieved will not need to be relearnt, we just move on to the next and then the next until we understand the lessons in full.

Each time we move up the ladder finally achieving to complete everything in detail. Then new situations arrive and off we go again. This we do over and over, life after life, often playing out situations with the same family members with rolls reversed.

Now I would like to talk about something different, Joy.

Joy is foremost boundless, for it is the best feeling you can ever experience here on EARTH. It is in the running with love, loyalty, and honour.

Joy is the most frequently felt feeling, giving a special jubilation of energy to any situation that completes itself wonderfully. It is life giving at its best. We grow from each and every situation and understand ourselves more fully. It is like completion.

We share this with many souls this lifetime, day after day.

Joy is associated with our body parts. It is often said joy is the blood of life and as so indicates a barometer of the blood. No fun and joy in your life, often represents a lack of blood or healthy blood types. This we have seen time after time. There needs to be a great fulfilment of time to embrace the happy side of life to bring the joy in and play with it.

We seek to unfold the honour attached to the karmic lesson. A karmic lesson is not always about correcting the wrong, quite often the opposite as it brings joy associated with it. We all tend to forget the lovely parts of our day and remember the difficult times. This is what we refer to as human traits.

Joy is pure pleasure and should be enjoyed to the maximum. Joy brings out your inner child. So let your child play, it will be the best experience you ever have. It will keep you young and ageless. We approve of dancing and swaying with the music and letting your heart soar. This feeling is beautiful and should be honoured as often as possible. We have our own brand of music, using our vibrations to soothe each other as it is often the best way we communicate.

I believe we have a lot in common with the humans. We don't have to bother with a lot of proprieties like eating and dressing, and working just to provide for ourselves.

We have it all in one, it is so easy for us, our feet are firmly planted to one spot providing all our requirements and we have strong skins to protect us. We love the same as the humans, and we trust the same. We are kind and generous and giving of heart. We do not have a voice most can hear, but if you really tune in its there.

We feel what you feel.

Sometimes it's frightening to watch you go through your lessons. There are days when we share in all your glory, and your joy. Being around you is what matters most of all to us. We enjoy sharing your lives and watching you grow as we to grow, in all our enthusiasm.

This is a beautiful time to be here on our planet as we whiteness the changing of energy's between the light markers and ourselves. The light markers are the crystalline energy that is changing our world. You may not realise this is happening on a daily basis, although it is, and is the way of the new millennium.

We will indeed realise on our return home, how far we have come.

We will be impressed with our outstanding ability to have been part of this amazing process. The new crystalline energy is affecting all of us the humans and the trees, and all the other souls. Those who did not wish to be a part of the new transition are currently preparing or have already returned home. This lesson was not necessary for them to be involved in. We respect this was not for everyone.

Time-honoured traditions were honoured by everyone and NEW ORLEANS the place in the last century to live it gracefully. The people from the north met the people from the south and paved the way. Life was not always smooth, but they worked it out. NEW ORLEANS is a special place, which won many hearts and is dearly loved by the people who live there, and the generations of families, that followed to this very day.

We are grateful for those who came before us, for we are embracing their lives as well as our own. We have learnt many things from their disposition and the trails, that they faced living here on this planet. This is a time of rapid change for us all and we must enjoy every given day, for the blessing it is. We honour ourselves to keep our journeys going. This is the ride of a lifetime for us and we wouldn't miss it for the world.

Would you like to share a past life story with us CHARLTON?

Yes, I have one of a heroic event.

I was a traveller in early times when travel was not an easy event. I travelled through hostile territory many times but this was an event that I never forgot, harrowing to say the least. I was ambushed and shot, left to die by the side of a road. I was travelling alone and didn't stand a chance really, it was days before anyone came by, but then a family came along in a wagon and tried with all there heart to save me. It took many days before my fever broke and I woke to find these lovely people had worked hard to keep me alive. I was so grateful, every day after that I grew stronger as we travelled on. I was asked to stay with them as we all had a better chance together to stay alive.

We travelled on perilously north to what seemed a better life ahead for all of us.

We became the best of friends and protected each other. Fever came as we approached other communities and travelled on. The father of the group passed away due to the fever, the rest of us survived. I became the leader of the family so to speak, to protect the wife and daughters until the son was old enough to lead. We encountered many hostile events, where I taught everyone to shoot and protect them selves. Then love came in a grand gesture, the eldest daughter and I became close and wed. This was the most amazing part of my life, as I never thought I would feel the love of a wonderful woman, one I had taught to be strong and defend herself.

We reached a place where there was land for all, our promise land. We all stayed together as that was how we worked. We had beautiful strong, vital children and raised them accordingly. I was their hero for getting them to where they were safe.

But most of all they were my heroes, one that gave me the gift of life.

Some lives stay gently on your mind to honour the people who gave you love and kindness. This is truly a beautiful gift.

Always cherish the love you receive.

Charlton.

Cellest

Hello I am CELLEST. I would like to add to *the book* to help you understand the difference between our souls and yours.

I am a small tree in the NEW HEBRIDES, small but ancient, in the order of one thousand of your years. We are situated in strong natural surroundings, where as yet no humans have passed. We are good with communication and hear all that we wish too. We send love to this planet and all inhabitants on a daily basics, hoping to increase the love, as that is what, we all came here to achieve.

I am enjoying my life free from strain and progress. I am living and supporting myself in the way in which I intended.

We, the trees are peaceful beings of light with a beautiful soul who descended to this planet for the purpose of growing our souls to learn the physical aspect of life.

Our souls are exactly like yours. There is no difference between us. We are you and you are us. We are all on an evolutionary journey to succeed, to find our own purpose, and live it well.

No matter what you find to do in your life, it will always be part of your learning ability. It can never be wrong, as it is exactly what you need to fulfil your path and follow your purpose. One doesn't have only one path to walk as we do many things consistently, which all add up to where we need to be, to get the right outcome.

Most of us have many fingers in the pie as you say. We have several dozen things on the boil at any one time. We play many hands in all different directions to give us the vital information we need to continue at full speed so we get the best outcome every time. This we do easily and tirelessly throughout all our lives. Time after time and life after life.

We set many goals each life before we come, and we try to exercise as many of these things as we can, never knowing if we will succeed at most of them because whether we do or not, does not really matter as we have many more life times to achieve this.

We are here to do our best and that is all we can ask of ourselves.

My goal this life is to help as many as I can. I am a leader tree. One who helps our young, but I also have qualities to lead our friends back home as well. My soul can lead them in the direction of home, when they are unable to find their way. Sometimes their lives are terminated quickly, leaving them feeling abandoned.

I escort their souls safely home and return for myself. This is my special gift.

This is a beautiful gift, one that is most appreciated by all who need it.

Now I would like to talk about sharing. Sharing is a lovely quality to have. It also is a gift in its own way. When one is able to give to another like they would to themselves.

This truly is a commendable quality to have. It shows love and respect for both of you.

Sharing is a wonderful thing and brings much happiness even if it's a bite of someones sandwich, it really is the thought that counts. When you share you favourite things it shows how much you trust each other. Trust is what makes the world go round, and that is what makes the world a nicer place. We all need to a little extra hand some times.

Time management is another thing we see you have difficulty with and we understand it simply isn't easy on anyone. We would like you to relax a little with it and we know some time slots have to be adhered to or you may miss your plane trip home. However at other times if you could relax a little where things are not quite so important. Life will flow much easier and time will be relaxed with you.

Time and timing is important but try not to allow this to rule your life. Life is meant to be pleasurable and kind. We did not come here to be stressed all the time. So take a breath and realise we came here to enjoy ourselves too. Love is the kindness we are made of, so share the love as much as you can.

I wish to keep living this life as I appreciate this opportunity to finish my journey to its end. I made a solemn decision to return to Earth at this time of the light transition to help it run smoothly. We are kind beings of light just as you are.

This will finish a charge I started quite some time ago, to stay till the end of the crystalline development. All our cells are currently being changed to crystalline DNA, so our bodies are strong enough to stay through the changing of light bands. Without this process none of us would survive, as the old cells would not be strong enough to go through this transition as Planet Earth moves through the solar system to where she needs to be. There are some who decided not to stay the distance with this and are concluding their lives here, as this had nothing to do with their journeys here.

We have many special gifts among us, one is we always include each other. We love one another. We do not hold bias towards our brother souls, as we consider ourselves attached to each other like a soul family. We all know that many of us are in fact family members and very good friends that are inseparable when we return home to spirit. This makes this time here all the more valuable to us as we are descending here all together to enjoy our lives and learn our soul lessons that we put before ourselves this lifetime. We are all grateful for the opportunity to be here at this given time.

We are all given time to process our thoughts, life hands us many trials at times.

Grief is one of these things. It takes the time it needs too. It is not a process that can be rushed, or it will rear up again and again until we deal with it or until we understand the process involved. So we recommend you to take your time to grieve your loss and understand the lesson you put before yourself this lifetime.

Cherish your memories or work through any issues that may arise, sometimes there is left over residue from the loss. Anger, frustration, and resentment can all be relevant. Give yourself time to grieve and heal. Every situation is different so please be patient with yourself, don't expect miracles strait away. It will come with the passing off time. Be gentle on yourself, and time will take care of the rest.

One of the greatest qualities one can have is to speak your truth, now this isn't the same for everyone. Speaking your mind isn't the same as speaking ones truth. Your mind sometimes can be ego based, ego is often conditioning passed down through generation after generations, and can be what everyone else expects is right in the circumstance. This is not always the best thing as it is not your truth.

Your truth is what feels right for you. It is not any one else's opinion or beliefs that matter here, only yours. Follow your heart and you will understand the difference.

Would you like to share a past life story with us?

Yes please, I have a beautiful life story to share.

I was a Queen to my King in EGYPT, in the early days. We wed with love on our minds. Some did not approve as they wished an arranged marriage for him with a stranger he did not know. He maintained marriage between two people worked best if love was the reason you were brought together.

We enjoyed our lives immensely, and were blessed with a son, a future King.

While the King was away on duty, I was kidnapped by the palace staff and taken away with my child to a lonely location for several months. This was very distressing, as I knew they lied to him about my whereabouts. I knew he would never give up on myself, and our son. He searched and searched for us to no avail it seemed, until one day he meet a beggar in the street who wanted to talk to him. This was not allowed, as he was the King.

In the dark of night he found his way back to the beggar, who enlightened him to a conversation he heard about the Queen. He said it wasn't clear to him where she was, only that she was alive and being held against her will. He knew these people came from another area so the King set out to find his Queen, and left no stone unturned.

After one month in the area a person gave him a tip off. Later that night he and his troops stormed the building and he himself rescued us. What a glorious sight to be saved by the man who loves you so much. We were taken to a safe place, fed and clothed. The next day journeyed home together. I marvelled at his sight, as he never gave up on us.

There were palace changes after that; my son and I had guards placed around us when my King was not present. We knew we loved each other with all our hearts and no one can come between two hearts that are melded together for always. Much love.

Cellest

Morgan Fay

I am a leader tree of many facets, many guises for this lifetime. I am in fact a ventriloquist of sorts. I am a multitasker in this life. I transcend this life into other planes of existence, and have several lives running at the same time. This is unusual as most others are not able to do this. I am millions of your years in age and have lots of experience in this field.

I belong to the fairy realm. I am an elemental, I am a light worker with great experience and one who cherishes life to the maximum.

Let me explain, I transcend too many places at any given time, this solar system and many others. There are many portals of which to visit, where we conduct lives in a sequence to the same life of existence here, running several lives at any given time. This is exciting for me, for I enjoy the level at which I have become familiar with and understand completely. I am originally from the fairy realm, that is where my roots are but I have progressed so far in many lifetimes of service.

I have enjoyed many lifetimes in different locations all over this galaxy. Sometimes resting in between to gain momentum before taking a leap off faith once again.

I wish to learn as much as I can, and also to be of help to others.

Being a tree this lifetime, has tremendous pull in the universe and will help me to learn what it is like to be able to help Mother Earth, as she follows her protocol of life. She has much to adhere to, to stay in line so she keeps her position in the solar system otherwise she will not stay in the right place and be swept away, by unnatural forces. This is a big job in any ones language and the help we give, keeps her on track.

We also provide life for the humans with the air you breathe. We find it ironic that our value here is understated. One day we will be sacred as otherwise you will not be on this planet at all. That is still a learning kerb for you all, when all native nomadic tribes knew this from the start. We find it hard to believe that you ignore the greatest gift that was ever given.

Modern ventures think they can override the protocol of life. We will watch and see. We watch with bated breath, there is only one outcome. Love is all there is.

In my lifetimes, I have had many rolls to play, as you are aware, we come for the physical life to be able to play out rolls with each other, time and time again.

We find this changeling and delightful too. Your level of understanding now gives you the insight to now know, how this happens.

Where as before you were not versed to know the roll playing and repeat lives that are playing out around you. This appears to be common knowledge these days.

We all understand the power of each other, which is great sometimes and even though at other times we butt heads over issues that seem important at the time. Lessons arrive before our very eyes some days and stay till we play them out or learn what we need to know. If we fight it, it will show up for us to complete another time.

There are certain times in our lives when we are not capable of completing lessons, so we save them for another time when we are stronger to do so.

This also works in with our karmic lessons.

I would like to share a past life with you, and I will remember the sweet lessons involved in this life.

In a galaxy far from here many light years ago. I retained a membership of value from this life, one that always serves my memory well. I was a bookkeeper of sorts, in charge of a library of memories of elders past. It was a job I cherished to the full and eventually passed on to another as time went by. I worked in what you call the Akashi records department.

A time-honoured tradition of keeping the records of our lives. Each and every one of us has long lists of where we have been and where we are going. It was truly an amazing and privileged position to hold. Every soul in the universe has documented evidence of every life we have experienced, long or short. Each life is as important as the next one and grows our soul to gain more value each time around. At times we reach our level of satisfaction and rest for a while in between, giving us time to heal from the many life times we pursue.

This life was an amazing experience from start to finish. I was in charge during a period known as the fall, a very important part in our history.

I would help souls map out their new lives and as you do this, you go step by step with them almost living it with them. It is a very exciting process to be involved in, it is their decision how they would like their lives to unfold.

We like to try certain things we have never experienced before. The way we descend to this planet, who our families are this time and how we leave this planet are all vital components to a great life. All in all this one was one of my greatest achievements to date. Sweet memories are made of this.

I wished to tell my story in *the book* to help you understand our plight, as well as yours. We are you and you are us, we are all the same souls living our lives that serve us well, blow by blow we get to experience all the details that we longed to feel, see and touch, that is what it is all about. Experiencing the dream, the dream of life.

Changing the ordinary to extraordinary every time. Love and light to you all.

Morgan Fay.

Joanna

JOANNA found a connection with me tonight and this is what she has to say.

I am a specialist in my field. I came forward to this life for great reasons, one of course is to help this planet cope with the new healing energy.

There will be times of swift movement as she prepares to slip into a new position to sustain her for many light years ahead.

The second is to honour myself and play out the life that surrounds me at present.

I am a beautiful loving tree on the ISLE OF CAPRI. I am here to enjoy the scenery and to be of service to all who need me, whether it is our family of trees or to help this beautiful planet. We all do what we can to sustain her as our lives also depend on her decisions to stay aligned in the solar system.

We are forbearers of news to help her understand what is happening on the topside. We carry vibrations through the earth to the centre. She can translate our messages and understand exactly what is going on all around us, even to the point of visitors circulating us. We are her news forecast team, one that she can rely on. We have been doing this job for thousands of years now and we all get a turn during our lifetimes here to provide the information she needs to sustain her. It is a privilege to work with a true master.

Our MOTHER GAIA as she is known to you, is a gentle soul with huge responsibility and this is her charge this millennium.

One she is very proud to fill, this will put the stakes very high for her when she returns home.

This is a task needing endurance with a lot of longevity, but she has chosen well to fulfil this role and also enjoy the task put before her. We all honour her.

I am enjoying communicating with you all, as it is a privilege to be able to put our thoughts in writing so that we can tell you about our lives, as before this it has not been possible. We all recall our lives that we experienced as humans when we talk to you. We never thought it would be possible to be able to explain our lives to anyone, but we are enjoying this process, there are many of us who wish to speak in what we call the book.

Our past lives have become more valuable, as we explain the joy we experienced, here on this Earth and on other planets as well. There are great choices to choose from when you wish to descend into a physical life. It all depends on the lessons you need to learn to fulfil your charges, which add to the glossary of your life.

A charge is a great investment in your resume of life. Great accolades are given to those who try. Not only to those who succeed, but sometimes it is hard to accomplish the simplest of things, but also it is important that we keep trying.

We work our way up the ladder to complete our charges, and then we move on to the next new exciting challenge. This is the dream we all wish to experience, a dream of a lifetime. We are always happy to be able to return into a life, which serves our purpose, and play it out to the end. We are all, capable of this and find the result is exactly what we needed to learn.

Would you like to share a past life story with us?

Yes, I believe so. I was an amazing artistic, one with great talent. I was able to capture ones life on portrait. The people of that time loved my work and gave me much pleasure that I seldom did anything else. I painted, drew portraits, and did almost anything anybody wanted. It was my calling and I loved it, some of my work is still on display to this very day.

Looking back I made some mistakes also, I never gave time to enjoy myself with the little things in life that really matter. I never took the time to have a family of my own or got to experience the joy of a life's partner. That was my misgivings that life, one that I have learnt from. Life is about balance and the balancing act of being able to do more than one thing at a time. Too much of any one thing becomes an obsession, and obsessions rule your life completely.

There are times where we experience a life that is about one aspect, sometimes we are so good at it that we forget there are many other arrears that make up a life. So we push on never knowing our capability in the other areas.

Life is a trial, sometimes we do it well and other times we learn from it. This is the great lesson we all came to learn to work out. These lessons help us to grow our souls and that is our main purpose for our visit to this life. I hope I may have helped someone else learn from my mistake, to change their life so they too can enjoy the balance of life.

Learning from a life well spent is a great reward on our return home. Love and blessings to you all.

Joanna.

Gerald.

My name is GERALD. I am from a land you call ROMANIA. I am very honoured to speak so my words can be placed in *the book*. We are so pleased to be able to tell the stories of our life and times, to be passed on for all to share. We are delighted beyond words.

This is my story, as for all of us we grow to a certain age where we are sure we will survive, and then we proceed into our life's purpose. The one we designed for ourselves to learn to grow our souls. The one aim we came here to achieve, for most of us is longevity and a grand passion to be able to complete our journeys in full, although is not always possible, we do the best we can.

For myself it is a passion to serve the great MOTHER EARTH and be of any help that I can as she also gives us life in return. Life is a two way street. We see you with your young as they grow, they take everything for granted, food shelter and monitory gain.

The best idea is to teach them life is never easy, always be on the look out as life changes from one moment to the next, and never take things for granted.

We see society's spoilt children who would not be able to fend for them selves if they had to. This is not the correct way to teach them. They have to know how to support themselves. Think for themselves and act for themselves. We teach self-sufficiency so they can be proud of whom they become and be self-reliant. This is the greatest tool any parent can give to a child, learning to develop choices that lead to a happier lifestyle. Thinking for them does not teach them to make their own decisions. Our job is to guide them so they learn to develop into the best version of themselves. This is what life is all about, teaching others what we too learnt.

We watch as time goes by and see the difference in our planet. We see so much has changed and it will be forever changing as the love on this planet grows more strongly. We will see people trust one another more, love one another more as this what we are trying to achieve, one step at a time. People are especially wary of each other, as trust has to be earned. It is a privilege to be loved by another. This is not just a given thing. In our world trust is assured, as we are not likely to beat each other up, and walk away and leave one hurt and alone.

Words also cut people down and debilitate their actions. These are the lessons the humans are learning, great lessons to evolve around. It is so much better to love than to hurt and hate. As time goes by more people will evolve into kinder human beings and love and trust will be top of the list.

On the grounds of personality, wisdom, and friendship may I say how well everyone is doing? We are extremely proud of how far you have all come. As we see it, your lives change every hundred or so years, a lot less sometimes and in each life you start at the beginning growing from an infant, to an adult. This takes a quota of time and yet you are still willing to do it all again and again. We greatly admire your ability to go round one more time. We see everyone progressing along at his or her own pace, making strong headway. Your souls journey to grow along with your lives is amazing.

We too enjoy this freedom as we grow our souls and also enjoy a resting life.

We have it all in one place, our piece of EARTH in which we reside, with all that we need at our fingertips or roots as it maybe. We are the warriors of light, travelling between light bands to experience this life in this time zone. We are here this life to witness the changing of the times, to change from the old to the new in record time. Those of us that are here at this given moment are all warriors, from times past, now witnessing and readdressing the new millennium in which will carry us into the new catalyst through time.

Our soul understands this, even if in this life we are absent at remembering every detail of our request from heaven. We are on the right path always remembering that, if we are still here, then we are working our way through our lessons to conclude that which we need to learn, from this as well as any other life we choose.

We are beautiful beings of the zodiac, no matter how far we roam, or how far we have come. We are always part of this great empire and part of the creator's hand. Thank-you, for allowing myself the joy of adding to *the book* I send light and love to everyone.

Gerald.

Whittsimonds.

Hello my name is WHITTSIMONDS and I am from a place you call MONTREAL. It is a cold climate, and one I enjoy immensely. We are designed for the weather here and appreciate our calling to help our great MOTHER EARTH where we assist in the process of life. I am very grateful to be able to add to *the book* It is a great opportunity to express ourselves and write the stories of our lives, so we can live on, in the hearts of those who choose to read our words. We consider this an honour.

I wish to talk about patience as this also goes along with love and honour. Patience sometimes seems like a test even to the greatest of us and comes in many forms.

It turns up at most every corner of our lives and is frustrating at its best, however this is our greatest lesson, and the hardest one to obtain at times. It seems to always be there to prove a point, and it turns up mostly to slow us down and make us rethink our plans or our pathway.

Patience is like dragging out time or so it feels, sometimes we gallop ahead of ourselves knowing this is where we are going and where we need to be, but it is too fast for others. So we are left to slow it down and wait until their process catches up.

This is very difficult for those of us who have the need to finish what we start. It is our greatest teacher and finding patience is not always easy, but it eventually teaches us that other people's experiences are not the same as ours. We would like to rush it through and get to the finish line and now we learn to slow it down and go with the flow. Then we achieve what it is we need to learn and have more appreciation the next time around.

I would like to talk about healing. There are many ways to do this to enhance our own lives. Speaking to someone nicely with respect is a healing quality not only for yourself, but also for the receiver. It makes them feel good about themselves.

There are a million ways to heal, listening to someone when they need to talk out their problems. Caring is also healing. Holding someone is healing, hugging them, touching them, and just drying their eyes, as they need to cry. It doesn't have to be rocket science just show them <u>love</u> every time.

Letting go of anger, blame, and resentment is a very healing process for your body.

Friendship is also a healing quality as it is based on love. Crystals are a great tool to heal with as they are directly from MOTHER EARTH and carry the EARTHS vibration with them. Medicines that came from our EARTH and the plant realm heal extremely well.

Healing comes in many forms, using your hands to heal is very popular. Healing with your guides, guardians and angels is beautiful way to heal your inner self.

Massage works very well as healing hands work to free up mussels that are stressed.

Forgiveness also works very well, forgiving yourself first and then others, heals your heart centre.

Letting go of old issues that plague us is extremely healing to our fine bodies, which struggle to hold old information that is redundant in our lives. Letting go brings rapid relief.

A smile is the most beautiful healer there is, a simple smile can wipe away sadness in a moment.

Singing is healing as it gives us pleasure to release our day-to-day stress, finding the best way to release and bring happiness to others as well. The list goes on and on, see how many others you can find as well.

Saying I love you to someone else is the best thing any one can ever say, as it heals your heart centre and theirs.

Would you like to add a past life story?

Indeed I would, I experienced a life of nobility where I was raised and given a title of a prince. I was given too many things and much privilege including education, travel, and guidance on all levels. I never knew what it was like to just be myself, it's not something anyone can teach you, it's something you must experience for yourself by trial and error, however no one would ever leave me alone long enough to experience anything for myself.

As I grew older I yearned to sail on the big ships and the KING granted me passage. It was a great place for me to learn my place in life. Here everyone was important, as it was all hands on deck. I just loved it where it did not matter to anyone who you are or where you came from. I learnt and loved the ways of a sailor. I was able to join in and be myself and learnt who I really was, not that royal spoilt brat.

We sailed and dropped cargo in every important port around the globe. I enjoyed being a normal person being responsible for myself. I drifted back home every now and then only to be told I couldn't leave again. It was in my blood by then and suited my way of life, something I couldn't go without so I eventually left, never to return.

I worked my way up the ladder and became a captain. My family never forgave me.

I worked hard and enjoyed my life my way. I had a family and children and never shared my secret with anyone to this very day, a life of fulfilment. All my love.

Whittsimonds.

Nathaniel

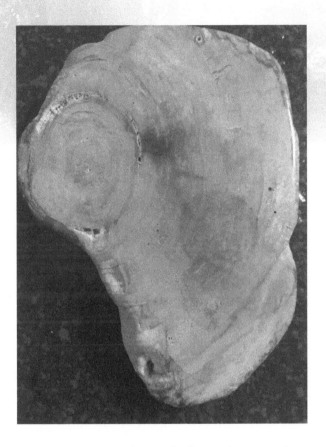

I connected to a piece of petrified wood to see if a connection was possible, and to my amazement these are the words I was given.

I would like to start at the beginning of my time. I was alive many centuries' ago living the life as a beautiful tree with love and respect for all. You were right, there is still life in us even though the life we lived is over. We have great memories of this life and many others, as my trunk or body descended into the earth to break down it was wrapped in warm earth, this nurtured my trunk and kept it all together, and as time past instead of breaking down I was kept immortalised in perfect condition, which became pressed with the passing of time and the weight of the earth.

I became crystallised in time and able to keep my memory of this great life.

Sometime later, dug up and sliced into pieces, hence the piece you are holding in your hands right now.

I am happy to share my life and times. My life started so long ago way before anyone knew or understand the plight of the trees. We were here to enjoy our lives living our purpose and helping MOTHER EARTH go about her duties. We were valuable to her in the early days, knowing when and what to report, being able to help in any way we could. I believe I lived in Australia or somewhere very close to that. It was a dry, hot climate but I enjoyed it. We lived with all the animals large and small and we shared a close bond. My purpose was to relate to MOTHER EARTH who then used our information with the stars to plot a course to keep her aligned in the universe. We did look all leafy and beautiful but we had our work to perform and we did it well.

This piece of stone has my markings left inside of it, my DNA I guess. I still have memory and can connect to you so easily like it was all yesterday. I have given the right to publish my words so the world can see that even in times like this when all has turned to stone, I still have a memory of a life I loved so well. I can also remember lives in other times but for now we will focus on this earthen journey. We enjoyed our lives where we focused on sending love to all on a daily basis never knowing when our lives would conclude.

Eventually time comes to all of us here, as we are here for short periods of time, then off to try out other outlets to give us the finished product of growing our souls.

This is the sweetest of journeys when love is present and our souls sing from each experience we have. This past life has given me a lot of value helping our MOTHER EARTH as she gave us life in return. Life is always a two way street. I am sure if each of us were alone day in day out, life would not feel worthwhile, it would be a challenge just to stay focused as most of us thrive on friendship and love.

I am most honoured to be able to speak in *the book* as I am not even living the life as a tree on this planet at the moment.

I am immortalised in stone forever.

I am able to bring grace to whoever holds me and loves me. This is the power that I still have, and willing to share my vibration for the next aeons of time. Good evening GLENDA, my name is NATHANIEL. God bless you all.

Nathaniel.

Jamaica.

I am JAMAICA, I am from a strong, vibrant class of souls that frequently visit this planet in order to grow our souls to our full potential. We enjoy being here on this planet at this given time as it helps us to achieve the growth we need to master our conquests in order to achieve our charges in heaven. We step forward for this life as we love this planet and it also helps us achieve our goals in the challenge of being a living tree.

It is an amazing life here, where we learn all aspects of life, so we get to understand all that life offers. We are so grateful for the opportunity to express ourselves and write our stories in *the book*. We also learn the values of being one of the most beautiful trees that grace this planet at this given time.

I believe I am hundreds of your years in age and have much longevity to offer yet.

I am situated in RUSSIA. We are used to the cold climate. I am part of a family of trees that have been here for many generations, as we work on our souls growth. We value every given day as a chance to enjoy our lessons and participate in this wonderful world we have provided for ourselves, brought into being by inspiring thoughts that are fulfilled by the universe using the law of attraction.

We attract a thought or a wish and it is given provided, we let the process proceed, if we rush this it fails to arrive at all.

We have beautiful thoughts and then let the universe provide it for us, and when we least expect it, there it is in all its glory.

Imagining it is already here works perfectly also. The law of attraction works well if we follow our heart and allow it to come naturally.

We heal ourselves from our heart centre, bless a limb if it has been severed or sweep love through each vein that is losing vitality and let it go. We have the power to regenerate in most cases and move on. In the event we die as you put it, we simply fade out and return to source, feeling the love from our loved ones who wait for us as we experience this life. We never die as such, our soul always moves on while our earthly bodies decay back to earth like you're saying ashes to ashes, dust to dust.

We then examine our life here and learn from any misgivings that may have arrived. We do not think harshly of ourselves, just endeavour to do better next time. We have things to complete and if we don't get it all done in this life then, we fracture it in the next time we return for a life. It is important we pick it up another time.

We do this time after time until our lessons are complete here and then move on to another life, where we are needed. We never die, life is always continuous. I believe you call it eternity. We like that word. It is very respectful.

I wish to add a past life story.

I was a stonemason in olden times, chipping out letters in rock, an art mostly lost these days as modern vices take over. I made a fair living in those times, it is a timely art handed down through generations of knowledge. I sincerely enjoyed my work and it provided well for my family. Some of the tombstones are still in existence to this very day. As a child I used to visit my fore bearers and watch how they worked with stone. I was truly amazed and drawn to the profession, watching in every detail as they carved each letter inscribing a person's life story, which was put into tiny letters to justify their whole life. To me, it truly was amazing and the families were so grateful, as this was the last request they could offer to their loved one.

This job taught me the value of living, and enjoying each and every given day.

Try not to engage in life's dramas and to live each day like it was your last, the best day you ever had. If you take the time to always find the best in someone, or something, revel in it, it will be the best, life has to offer you each and every day.

Draw the best conclusion and then you can relax, and let the rest flow naturally. Your life will start to flow in all the best directions and everything you want will flow unto you. This is the law of attraction at its best. NAMASTE.

Jamaica.

Gerrico.

Hello! I am GERRICO. I am honoured to be able to reach you. I wish to add my story to *the book*, I live on a large rocky mountain.

I am one of many and I am tall and strong and have learnt the value of going with the flow. I have many valuable years of lessons under my belt, as you would say, that we have learnt by choosing this life. It is the best way to work out our lessons until we become complete with the process. This process is ongoing, we deal with one thing at a time, and we see the humans have to deal with many processes at any given time. We are in awe of how well you work out everything, it must be mind blowing sometimes.

I am a leader tree, one who helps our young. We all have a purpose to follow and are committed to fulfil the journey we have chosen. I am now large enough to send vibrations through to central EARTH, where our data is stored and used when needed. It is a little bit like your I- cloud method where you store things until needed. We are able to send vibrations on all aspects of life, we monitor the soil, weather and water use, temperatures around us, and all activity radiating around us.

The EARTHS central control then has a handle on what life is doing on the topside.

This information is continually updated and helps MOTHER EARTH stabilise her position in the universe.

We are born to succeed, to not look back, and to be excited at what is in store for us.

We are in charge of our own destinies and it takes time for all of us to realise we are what we think, good, bad or ugly it will come as a matter of what we put out there.

Most of us take time to get this, the same with the humans, the ones who understand this seem to get many more things coming their way a whole lot quicker, and their life is a much happier one indeed.

Privacy is one thing not previously touched on in *the book*.

Privacy is your birth- right and your privilege, it is not something someone else should spoil for you. Those who choose to undermine you are in fact creating karma of their own doing. It does not have anything to do with you, however a sense of betrayal is often felt. These are the lessons we are all here to learn and master. Life after life we start to learn this well and enjoy the benefits it brings.

Timing is not always about being on time. Timing is the process with which we follow in our lives. We know when it is time to move on and not dwell over things we cannot change, if we don't change our opinions, we lose our dream. Our dreams are so important they keep us alive, they keep us on track and our life sizzles with direction. We feel on fire as you say, it is then we know we are heading in the right direction and life feels worthwhile.

When you loose your mojo you lose your direction and your self-esteem.

Feel in your soul when it is time to move on and act accordingly otherwise you are losing valuable time and time is of the essence, or life just passes you by.

Trust your heart when your head is unable to make a decision, your heart is never wrong. Follow your own guidance and you will never look back. Life really is that simple, it was not meant to be a struggle. Trust yourself and your feelings and life will become the best show on Earth. Your show, your way, trust you can do it.

Past life story to share.

I spent a life travelling with a circus, where we all helped in any way we could.

We helped with the travel, to erect the tents, feed animals, and provide the show. We were like one big family. Life was tough in those years there was not a lot of work available, so one did anything to survive and together we did it well.

I was especially good working with the big cats, I looked after them very well, but I did not do the show with them. They worked well with the master and I was their saving grace, I loved them so much. They knew the difference between us, I was their keeper and enjoyed their company. We trained their young from their early days and gained their respect, they felt like they were my own family. I was so drawn to them, they were the delight of my life.

We travelled most of our lives and in between we did shows, where I met a lovely woman who joined our crew as a dancer. We fell in love and spent many years together, staying with the circus as that became our lives. We were never sure where we would settle and so we stayed until the end of the circus. I took the cats with me, as I could not bare them to go to anyone else in case they mistreated them. They lived out their days gracefully. It became my purpose to love and provide for them. I truly was their friend and companion throughout their lives. It was a great privilege and one I will remember always, it stays gentle on my mind. I send my best regards to you all.

Gerrico

Godfrey

Hello, I wish to speak tonight, I am GODFREY, and I am from SPAIN. I am a trusted elder here on the peninsular. We are very revered as our lives have spanned for more centuries than anywhere else in Spain. My next lifetime, I hope to make it to a Sentinel. This will be an amazing feat to finish, one I started a very long time ago. Then I will be free to make other decisions that will go in other directions.

I am a long range forecaster with weather conditions. I always understand the tides and times and know exactly what is ahead of us. This is my speciality and I absolutely love my job.

I wish to talk about forestry and replantation. We know because we can see what is happening, this is our life we are talking about. This time it is our choice to see if we can live to our potential and finish our life purposes as we planned too, in the first place. We didn't understand how hard this life could be when we first came, as it is the same for all of us, you included. We didn't understand that if we were sitting in an exact spot and the humans denote a road needed to go there then, we are gone strait away with out a leg to stand on. Many of our lives have been taken in the interest of your roads not withstanding houses and building. It is a hard endeavour for us just to be here with all the rules that are applied these days. For the ones that are left like myself it is pleasure and pain, the pleasure is in living on this beautiful planet every day. It is astounding and we go about our lives as we should, and then there is the pain we feel for those of us who do not make it, who never even got a say, they were just removed and thrown on a pile to rot.

How harsh that is for them as well as us who are left to bear witness to this ordeal. <u>We would like to rebel at the way we are treated</u>. It is the humans who will suffer at their own hands in time as the oxygen decreases on this planet, and there is nothing that replaces us, or the job we do.

Deforestation threatens all our lives, we understand it is the generations that came before you that have done the damage. We would like to see more forests started so as to rebuild what has been taken, you really need to apply yourselves to this quickly as time will run out.

The way we see it, we think your problem is, your monetary system has to be accounted for every time something has to be done and therefore fail to achieve the target. Each and every one of you is capable of planting more trees and scrubs to achieve more oxygen for yourselves, it really is that easy. If everyone helps a little, it will go a long way in the right direction. Think about us and change your thinking, it will benefit every one in the long run.

I am telling it like it is in the endeavour it will help some of you, to understand our feelings and our plight. Just publishing this book is the greatest step forward we can ask for right now, as we make our feelings known to the world. We are all grateful for the chance to show case our words. We are also very proud of ourselves for being patient enough to work through our vibrations to change it to your word forms. We also thank GLENDA, as this process is not an easy one. She also struggles with this challenge, it is not easy to be the one, who puts their life on the line so we can tell the world how we feel about everything, we are truly grateful indeed.

Time is very important, your time and ours, every day is a blessing. We only get so many, and our time is up. We try very hard to be love and send love very moment of the day, it is so important we don't waste a minute. Any time lost is never given again it just passes us by, so always try to fill your life with meaningful things that matter to you, because you matter most of all. Do the things that bring you joy. Joy should be a great part of each and every day. Laughing and smiling count to, smile your way through life and life will become a breeze and your burdens become few.

We see you struggle with life's challenges, we too struggle sometimes with decisions that are made on our behalf, or so they say, except we do not get a say, we are just removed in an instant. Condemned to silence and no choice given. We return home in a panic not knowing sometimes what happened, and then we are counselled until we understand all the facts and accept the outcome. It is always final, and then we are free to heal and move on, and get on with our lives and try again if we wish.

I am looking forward to my next life as well as I have done a great number of lives and am very close to receiving my masters award, which will rank me as a Sentinel on my next journey.

I would very much like that award as a Sentinel as that will take me to a much higher realm in the future. This is the goal I hope to achieve. My own life's purpose if you like.

Past life Story

I was born in an era of great triumphs, we sailed the seas and were discovering land in other areas, our boats were not strong in those days and we didn't have any way of knowing about the weather, except charting the stars at night and hoping we would survive. We saw the great whales on our journey and that was a beautiful omen for us as we figured if they could live this far out we too would be safe. Sometimes we sailed for weeks at a time not seeing land and then finding an island some inhabited and some not. We were great heroes and didn't even know it at the time.

I guess it was adventure at its best, charging forward and not thinking of what could happen. Some of us returned to our homeland while others stayed to start new lives in exciting new places, overall a great outcome and a great life, one that stays gently on my mind. Love and blessings from

Godfrey.

Chatsby

Hello I am CHATSBY. I am a revered member of the tree realm here on this beautiful planet at this given time. I am here to embrace life and love, just like everyone else.

I am delighted to be able to speak tonite, we all wait in the hope we can tell our story and hopefully make a difference to help the humans understand we need each other to survive here.

Every one of us makes a difference, even though we may not feel like we contribute anything to the universe, just know that you do. Your choice everyday counts very much in everything you do, so it would be wiser to be happy in every given situation as this makes everything move faster for you, just this tip alone is a great one. When you are sad you slow your own process down and limit the outcome. Everything you want is moving towards you at a great rate, only you have your finger on the control button, no one else is in charge of your life.

We allow others to guide us or define us and we should not allow them the privilege, as this is our life to do however we wish. They have theirs and they should get on with looking after themselves and leave us to ours. This is our greatest lesson and we mostly do not acknowledge it in our lives every day. We don't even see it but there it is right under our nose. The number one lesson, <u>do as you wish to be done by</u>, try it and you will see your life improve the very first day and every day after.

It will be a remarkable change and one that will make you feel better about yourself and feel more loved in return.

I am a peace provider here on this planet. I help our tree souls to cope with all aspects of life, some struggle with the lesson they came here to master and I assist them to feel the love in the situation and allow themselves to learn to go with the flow as the humans say, and allow the process to come into balance, just taking a breath and allow all to be as it is, usually works wonders. We all worry and worry doesn't achieve anything except to make us ill or upset. So consider it a wise point and do not allow your ego to take control as it never is as bad as it seems. We all learn later that it is a waste of time and causes heartache and grief. When you cease to worry, your life improves immediately.

I myself never wallow about anything, it is what it is and no one can change the outcome, if it is meant to be then it will be. Acceptance is all that is needed.

We are all here to help our great MOTHER EARTH in the cycle of life. Every decision has an outcome and we are all here to play our part in learning our souls growth and every thing we do in our lives also impacts directly or indirectly with the vibrations of the EARTH.

Currently there are more people here than ever before, as we are here for the changing of the light bands. There are great happenings taking place around our planet and solar system and while we cannot physically see this with our naked eye, it is a big event one that goes down in history, and by that I mean in the AKASHI records department of our lives and our planets life. We are being rewarded extra points for our time here at present as it is a special vocation we all agreed on to be part of, a special moment in time.

Now I would like to give thanks to our friend GLENDA for having a go, this is a greater task than even she can understand at present. We all have important things to achieve this lifetime and this is the task she chose to try to do with all her heart. These tasks we undertake are sometimes not possible in this life we have right now, so we save it for another life, if fate plays a dealing hand and we do not feel safe to do so. It matters not when we do it, so long as we try to fit it in another time around.

We are very blessed as we feel she will accomplish the books and help everyone accept; We are all one. Our souls are exactly like your souls, there is no difference between us, only the guise we choose this lifetime. We wish you love and peace during this lifetime, think fondly of us as we do you. Cherish each other and give love your best shot after all. Love is what matters most in this life of ours.

I wish to add a past life story.

I was a man of many talents during a lifetime of strife and trouble in the very early years. I was a soldier in a war zone in which the fighting was fierce and as always we were never given a choice, if you were young and strong, then you were expected to be there to fight for your country.

I was clever and had a better understanding of how things worked. I was taken from the field and given a chance to lead an army, to outwit the enemy. We did many manoeuvres in many places and finally regained our land in a promised position, which held it for many years to come. We learnt to plan our battle procedures and ensured a strong hold instead of running blindly into the enemy, this made me a hero of the times. Planning strategies was a surer outcome and saved many lives.

We progressed well and never lost a battle or our land. Some of these ideas are still used today, however modern ways are now more efficient.

Still, a life well lived and respected to this very day. Much Love.

Chatsby.

Chantilly

Hello, I am CHANTILLY I am an elder at this time on the planet, here to be of help to our great MOTHER EARTH as she realigns herself in the solar system so she can finish out her life as she planned. We are all passing by this lifetime, we are in and out of lives but this is not so for MOTHER EARTH as she spends aeons as one particular life and chooses to do this wisely and accurately. She will still be here long after we have all finished with this EARTH.

Firstly we must learn and understand the great lesson in love. Love is the greatest reason we are here for, to learn to give and receive of ourselves.

Love makes our lives very rich.

Love thy self than everyone else. We must understand this unconditionally before we can be of any help to others.

Tonight I wish to talk about differences, we are all the same but different if that makes sense. For yourselves you are all human, male or female, similar but different in many ways.

For us we are all the same but different as well. We can be of different families and there for do not look the same or have the same colours but we are still trees.

This is also true for yourselves as you are all from different nationalities and that makes you unique, but you are still human.

The differences I wish to talk about really is attitude, this is what counts the most and not the colour of your skins, where you live or what particular possessions you have.

Attitude is everything, whether we are happy or sad, nice to others with a kind heart, is what matters most of all. We all have a civic duty towards each other to be tolerant and kind. I am sure none of us like it when someone is unkind and rude to us personally.

It is paramount we all keep our cool and help each other as much as it is possible.

We all have differences to cope with in life and it is up to all of us to see we don't inflict our pain on to someone else, and ruin their day as well.

Take a moment to care about someone else's feelings and you will be rewarded and that is the difference. Caring is the best thing we can accomplish this lifetime along with loving yourself.

We gather information all year around that teaches us to bend with the wind and to not sway against it, for that would not work out very well for us. We would snap and it would cost us our branches and our branches are like family.

You call this going with the flow. Going with the flow is more productive and positive and it keeps us going in the right direction.

We are all working together to show it is possible as we all work for the good of our planet and ourselves. We invest wisely in our future and hope to create good vibes to continue our work. Our lives are ever lasting as we pass our duties on to our young to do the next round as they too hand it on at a later date. We pride ourselves to teach them everything they need to know in order to survive and learn how to keep MOTHER EARTH updated with the latest happenings around her.

We trust you are enjoying our words as much as we love being able to have them written on our behalf. This is indeed a privilege for us as we only use vibrations between ourselves and we have to apply this a little differently when we talk with our human friend. There is a little delay in the process while we find the words that match what we wish to say.

We are now becoming accustomed to the process and streamlining it to be easier and quicker. We are very privileged to be part of *the book*, which will help everyone understand us on a more personal level. We are delighted beyond belief, and proud of our lives and our past life stories. We never thought we would be able to share our lives in this way, as it usually stays in our souls memory, where we can access them when we return home or in another lifetime.

We write our stories in what you call an uncommon dialect, it is our version and quite often not written with your version of English, but we do our best to translate our lives on to paper. Much Love

Chantilly.

Silvester

Good evening, I believe I am your one to answer tonight. I have been sending you visions in the last few days to let you know I have connected to you.

I am proud to answer your call.

My name is SILVESTER. I am a large majestic tree in the PALUMA region in NORTH QUEENSLAND, AUSTRALIA. I absolutely love my position here in the rainforest atmosphere. I am a leader tree here in this district and pledged to guide our families of trees in any time of trouble or disharmony or to just be here to assist however I can. My family name is

MONTAROUS but in this life I choose my own name to honour my soul journey. I am fulfilling my lessons here as I planned.

I am a chosen one here to assist or give back to MOTHER EARTH. I have chosen to give a number of lives in the next few centuries to allow Mother Earth to complete her journey well and which will also honour my soul lessons that will take me to a higher level of existence the next time I plan to descend into a life. An award of master should be obtainable when complete. We all plan our lives a long way ahead of ourselves before we transcend, so we know our best route to obtain the accolades we wish to feel in this life.

Feeling! Is a beautiful way to acknowledge this life, so too is caring, consideration and nurturing. These are the major ones I am concentrating on this life and next time I will pick three others to guide my souls pleasure.

On this side of the planet we are responsible for certain tasks to help MOTHER EARTH perform her duties to stay ever present in her roll. Her life also affects ours as we wouldn't be here if it was not for her anyway. I myself have a certain time-slot to be her adviser, it only comes around a couple of times in our lives but we are geared to know exactly when that is, it is a privilege to serve a true master in her position.

We translate our positions to her and give the information needed. It is a bit like your latitude and longitude, we guide her through channelled information given to us from the star constellation, this is our purpose and when one of us is removed that is in our circle, it creates a void of destruction for all of us. We struggle to maintain equilibrium then we add a younger tree to start to teach our ways too, and so life begins again and again.

This we repeat over and over so MOTHER EARTH remains protected.

I hope I have explained this well enough as it isn't easy to put into words.

Our longevity is vital for everyone's sake, we can't get them to understand how important we really are. It is not just the oxygen its survival for all of us. We really do not want to fail as this will impede on all of us and no magic will save us then, we will all die prematurely. We will have failed at our attempt to live peacefully together.

So please give us a go, we are you and you are us, our souls are exactly the same as yours.

I send love to you, each and everyone of you, every given day. Love always

Silvester

This Tree and its Story is dedicated to CHRIS MacRAE as this tree gave great friendship and Love, each time he passed by.

Kosack

Hello! I am a living tree on the FRENCH RIVIERA. I am known as KOSACK. I am a tree of distinction and many centuries old. I am an old fella to most but I am wise and have learnt many lessons this lifetime that tie into my life's lessons, of which I came to work on this lifetime. My souls purpose is to live a great life and gain many distinctions on my return home, as this will raise my vibration to qualify as an elder. This is a great reward for me as I wish to move forward into new territory to work with the Akashi record department, you have to be an elder to qualify. It is imperative that you have to have many lives of experience before you are able to teach and advise others. I am looking forward to that challenge and know it will be so exciting.

I am a leader tree here at present to be of help to our brother\ sister trees to help guide them in times of trouble or grief.

Grief is a major one, we all suffer from grief at some stage in our lives, and it is how we handle it that matters most of all and how we come out at the end, understanding the loss or devastated and not able to cope at all. We work on raising self esteem to reencounter life as we know it and help them to be independent in their thinking process so life can be enjoyed once again. It is very satisfying to see the results when you are able to reach them and teach them to live again.

Death is only a change of form, however it is difficult to understand when we are here and do not bring all our memories with us this lifetime, so we must relearn and accept there is a greater purpose to our lives. We do know that life is indeed a miracle each and every day, it cannot be seen by the naked eye, it is felt deeply in our hearts where our soul resides.

We follow through many cycles in our lifetime hoping to be able to fulfil all we planned to do in this life, and sometimes it does not work out that way as the timing is not right, however we try and those lessons that we do succeed with are great and we enjoy the fruits of our labour. And if we do not finish everything we keep it for another time when that need becomes more important.

Then we finish it with all our heart and soul.

I myself enjoy my life here as it is glorious, but I do remember a time not that long ago really, when bloodshed fell at my feet, I guess I never really understood why people were made to kill each other over land that was never there's anyway.

Whichever way you look at it, it didn't belong to them personally or belong to the country that claimed it. Land does not belong to anyone it is part of our MOTHER EARTH and is a gift for all of us to share, sometimes I am not sure what the humans are thinking, only that they have a long way yet to understand the basic principles of existence. When the first nomadic tribes were on this planet they found a spot that suited their culture as far as food, water and shelter were concerned and moved when that or the climate didn't suit anymore. They knew it wasn't there's and they didn't need to own it. There is now a very real problem with this owning thing as more people move on to this planet than ever before and it starts to make a sub culture for those who have no wish to own a piece of land. For they are the smart ones really, they do not wish to be held back and are free to move, as they like.

I would like to talk about this owning thing, not one person or tree here owns anyone else, as this is a statement of conditioning that has passed from one generation to another. We are appalled at watching this happen, it happens in your partnerships with each other and in your governing powers that be. If you look in the animal kingdom you can see they do not own each other. They enjoy each other. We are here to live our lives the best we can and move on whether that is to another spot on the planet or return home with the knowledge they did the best they were capable of this life. Our lives do not have to be rocket science as you put it, we are here to live and enjoy this life as beautifully as we can knowing we fulfilled our soul purpose, it is not about becoming rich, and owning everything in sight. It is about being true to yourself, speaking your truth, loving who you really are, and having compassion for those who cross your path. It really is simple, keep your life clean and simple. This way you can sit back and enjoy everything and everyone that you come in contact with and really enjoy this game of life. That is the best-kept secret ever, just go with the flow and be your beautiful self. This is the best advise I can give you to start living your life in an amazing way, one that compliments you, because you are who really matters most of all. Thank you for the wonderful opportunity, to add to *the book*, GOD'S speed to you and yours.

Kosack

Jescinta

Hello! I am a fruit tree, my fruits are so sweet, they are used to make many different varieties of food.

I am so blessed that my fruit is so purposeful and provides nourishment to all who need it. I also supply food too many different birds and animal life, to help nourish their young, initially it was the birds that would eat the fruit and leave the seeds to prosper into young trees themselves, but now the humans are in on the deal.

They take the fruit away in large boxes and the fruit goes to all different places around the world sometimes, this gives my seeds the privilege to travel and grow in other places never dreamed of before, this spreads our seeds, far and wide.

My name is JESCINTA. I live on the eastern coast of AUSTRALIA. Mango is what you call me. There are many of us here in plantations and in the average back yardS, up and down the coast. The climate suits us here and we grow into quite large trees if left unattended, nature at its best. We are wise beings of light here for the same reasons as you, living and growing our souls and focusing on love, wisdom, and compassion just to name a few. We all came from other galaxy's far from here and had a multitude of lives in other places that served us well, but for now we are here to help MOTHER EARTH go about the changes so she can navigate her place in the new solar system, to be where she needs to be for aeons to come. When we leave this planet, we know how important our job was and revel in the excitement that we played a part, however small. It gives us such satisfaction on a job well done.

We love the excitement as each day dawns, it brings our lives into reality, that we are here to be of help to this beautiful planet and not forgetting we are able to help the humans as well. Most of us are healing trees and we are able to listen when anyone has a problem, we most certainly love a hug and know you are hugged in return. We wrap our heart and soul around you too. You can ask for a healing, we are very good at sending warmth into your body where there is soreness, lean up against us and ask for warming love to be sent to you; it really is that easy.

I myself am aware that your culture does not really believe we can heal, it seems to us that as you become more technology based you have forgotten your primal instincts and do not let yourselves feel what is important, you have forgotten we are all connected to one another.

We can prove this as otherwise we would not be able to have these words written on our behalf as this lady feels close to each of us and can feel our vibration we send to her. This is the sweetest gift we have to offer, sent with all our love. Let yourself feel what is more important in life, stay tuned as they say, otherwise you are missing out on the best life has to offer. Learn by holding a crystal first, feel the vibration it offers and then you will realise we are no different really. Just touching us reveals the same and as you feel us we too can feel your vibration in all its glory, we feel the love you have to offer us, and we are able to transmit our love to you also.

Life is a two way street and whether we understand it or not we are all souls on our evolutionary journey relating to one another. Sometimes the memory loss we start with here hinders us, but the whole point of the journey is to remember what we are capable of and see how much we can accomplish this life without knowing why, is truly amazing and gives the best results all round and when you return home you will be so proud of who you have become and the lessons you have accomplished. Every lesson well learnt will never have to be repeated again, you then go on to do other lessons until you master them all.

Then one day you will be rewarded for your work with the finishing a charge, which goes toward an honour of a master of whatever field you chose to fulfil. Like a master of evolution for instance, this takes many lives of dedication to accomplish. The reward is a wonderful experience and so on we go again, as life is eternal and we keep striving to gain the ultimate place for our souls pleasure.

I have so enjoyed talking to you all it has been my greatest pleasure to add my life and times in what we call *the book*. I hope every story here assists you to understand us, as we have learnt so much as well in adapting to human words. Love and the very best of wishes to you and yours.

Jescinta.

Rowan

I am a tree of distinction that resides in NEW CALEDONIA and I am a peacemaker here at this given time. We are all enjoying our time here, as this is what we all planned, to do until the changing of the light bands is complete. It is now the twenty first century by your calendar time and realigning will take many more years yet to complete, when that is done, there are many more phases to go through so MOTHER EARTH is always busy with the next thing on her agenda. She goes through lots of different phases and moves in her lifetime and it is important she follows her instincts and moves as protocol demands.

We all assist her, being her eyes and ears so to speak, we guide her every move.

We are all connected and there-for trust each other explicitly, our souls speak the same language. I guess you could say we are family. We are all here to experience different events that grow our souls capability to interact more perfectly.

Each time we descend into a life, we accept that we learn new things and grow from them. We choose different souls to play our life around, different places, times and scenes.

We star in our own shows playing the leading role.

I enjoy being here it is a real honour to be on this planet at this particular time as this is a challenging time for MOTHER EARTH as she moves in the solar system. We love our lives immensely and the changing of the seasons is indeed the most beautiful part of our lives, it is spectacular for some of us. We shed our leaves, it's a bit like out with the old and in with the new, and it makes us feel refreshed and relaxed. We follow the seasons as it gives us the lifeblood we need to pursue our goals and keep us moving in the right direction, that is why in the human life you need to set new goals and sometimes the changing of the seasons prompts these changes, new goals keep us moving forward and keeps our motivation at its highest level. We love a challenge and we see you do too. This is what keeps the life force in us at the highest level.

Our life force is the first layer in our aura, followed by many other layers, which become our auric field. Then our auric field is like a shield that is personal to us on all levels, it indicates levels to us if sickness is present, or simply someone becomes to close to us and enters our field enabling us to feel their presence and also their motives, as to whether they come with love on their minds or any other reason.

We immediately feel all impulses and know exactly what to expect.

When we feel threatened we react the same as you do, I think fear is the word you use, fear is a feeling of helplessness and leaves a residue that is hard to endure, given that it is not your own truth, sending love from your heart to the problem is the only way to deal with this emotion, until your thoughts come into alignment with the situation, then you can acknowledge the problem has been dealt with and love resumes once again. Love is the greatest gift in this life and every new day that dawns is a delight for us to share, spend your time being grateful for every opportunity that is given to you as it is sometimes, just a fleeting moment of a life well lived.

We wish to acknowledge the gifts we receive in the form of compliments to our tree families all over this planet, sometimes we are amazing in all our glory and at other times are pruned to perfection, planted to make special effects in tree lines, boarders etc.

We are always grateful for the opportunities we are given, as we all need each other here on this planet as we give life to each other. NAMASTE.

Rowan.

Shamual

SHAMUAL is a beautiful tree in HAWAII, who I met personally on my last visit, overlooking the sea where the tours take people to swim with the turtles.

Hello! I was very amazed to meet you that sunny afternoon, caught by surprise I guess you could say. I watch many people who arrive here daily with the tours and I can easily say without hesitation that no one has ever wrapped their arms around me and talked to me before, and as you know it took me moments to respond I was gobsmacked, but only for a moment.

I couldn't believe you were here with me, we do know you exist and that you are helping us here on the planet at this time. I felt so privileged and I was honoured to assist you with a healing that could send warmth to your chest area, as you had previously been sick with the flue. I could feel that straight away when your hands first touched me. You could feel my vibration and I yours, it is a wonderful gift to be felt by another soul who understands each other perfectly. I was truly grateful for our experience, even though it was a short visit.

I wish to talk about the soul journey, as that is what we are all doing here at this particular time, playing out our lives to enhance our souls journey. We live many different lives in order to learn and too feel everything, we go through, step by step we create the many episodes we need to learn from, to grow our souls, until we master it and move on to the next lesson. When we master it we no longer need to repeat it again, we have it saved for future reference. There is always more exciting lessons waiting for us to complete, and it never ends.

My job here is to relate to MOTHER EARTH as you know, as we feed information through to her, but it is also my job to teach the young on these levels so they too one day will be able to keep sending her information she needs to survive. Teaching our young is a never-ending process as they too will teach their young in due time, our lives are sedimentary compared to yours but our lessons still come through equally the same.

I am enjoying my time here, it is serene, and pleasurable I am close to the sea and enjoy the prevailing winds, this area enjoys enormous surf and people come from all lands to enjoy riding the boards on the waves. This must be very pleasurable for them as they keep coming every season.

I am a time-keeper here in this life, it is my job to be ever present for our souls who doesn't understand our time factor, we council them as sometimes they worry about the longevity of their lives and we teach them that it is not the longevity that matters most of all, it is important that they are here in the first place to greet their lessons head on and participate in their souls journey that they have chosen to fulfil.

We too go through a veil of forgetfulness when we descend or otherwise we would not be able to concentrate on the life at hand. We would not be able to enjoy our tranquil life if we remembered every part of each life we lived before. I think we would feel tormented by some of our early lives. We grow through each incarnation just the same as the humans do, learning more each time we progress, for some of us it is early days and others are reaping the benefit from many lives of progress which will add to a great accolade on their return home. It all adds up to a completion of a charge at sometime or another seeking a greater soul purpose, then ever before.

Our time here is never wasted even if this life does not pan out the way we planned. Every step is still important and never wasted. We give them the strength to continue, as we really never know when our lives will conclude, and for that we are truly grateful.

Would you like to add a past life story?

Yes thank-you

I was a warrior in an ancient times, we all rose to the call to protect our land and our people. The wars went on and on and it seemed there was always something to quarrel over, but we served our time and went on to live our own lives. I had a family of my own, and I was especially gifted with inventing tools and so made it my profession, I invented all sorts of garden implements to make life easier and went on to develop horse shoes. Well that hit the jackpot and I became a leading farrier and blacksmith, which was in great demand across the land.

I travelled everywhere teaching the art of making the shoes and fitting them.

I am so proud as they are still widely used to this very day. Nothing has superseded them at all. They have modified them to suit today's climate and material but the idea is still the same. My best effort yet as an inventor and has saved many horses hooves, and is now a time honoured tradition. I am very grateful I could share my story with you all as it is one of my most treasured memories of a life well lived.

Love and best wishes
Shamual.

Harmon

I am HARMON and I am a very large shade tree that grows wild and free in the hillside of OAHU HAWAII. We knew you were here and I wish to be the one that answers your call today.

I am part of the hilltop trees here in the mountain ranges that are seen rising on the other side of the island overlooking the beautiful beaches. Our view is suburb, we choose to go with the flow and are enjoying our lives immensely.

We often have visitors here around us as they film their stories using us as a background. I believe you call them movies, we had one imitating large monsters running through our trees pretending to be scary, even we had many smiles watching this, however we watch as they can be very harmful to our environment, especially the film crews and their gear. They have a lot of small machines (bikes I am told) that enable them to move fast through the bush to enable them to be different places faster. These leave tracks that are harmful out to environment.

I would like to talk about our comfort first, we all know you are starting to value us as beings on this planet, and we appreciate that very much, however we are leaving this planet faster than we can replace ourselves mainly due to the humans squatting on our land. Well we say our land as this was our birth-right first, to be wherever we are, and that's how we see it, that's how it is up here in the mountains, we are entitled to be wherever we are, to grow and nurture ourselves and reproduce as we wish, but this is not so down on the flat ground where you call towns and cities. This seems to belong to the humans now and we are removed if we are not in the right place according to them. We are chosen for our shape or size and only grown to enhance their buildings to give a look of nature around them. This is already pushing us out and they seem to forget who provides the oxygen they breathe on this planet.

We are at a all time low with oxygen now, but still they remove us, the large trees here should be revered and kept at all cost, they are not replaceable quickly, it takes many generations to grow to the large size needed to generate enough oxygen to be of help. Every tree removed places us backwards on the scale and at this stage we will never keep up. Please look at the destruction and think hard about it, give us both a chance to live. One cannot live without the other. We are all beings of light here to live our lives out peacefully to love and protect each other.

Do you wish to add a past life?

Yes indeed.

I wish to share one life I enjoyed immensely.

My name was MICHAEL and I became a saving grace in that life at the time, this life was on a planet called Lords, very similar to this planet where we spent time having lives to satisfy our soul purpose and enjoyed the lessons attached.

As I grew up and the only thing I wanted to do was to be a doctor and in those days being a sidekick was the only way one learnt, assisting the doctor, donating your time, and learning along the way. I was with the doctor some four years when there was a mine accident, a terrible time really because as the men were dragged out, not many of them survived and most of them were crushed or their lungs damaged from the gasses inside the mine. A horrible time for everyone there. I heard a scream come from the town folk who were assisting with the accident.

Doctor! Doctor! Can you come its Mrs PARRY she has gone into labour, at the mine there were no comforts around, too far to get her back to town and the doctor was too busy with the men.

He winked at me as if to say, go on so I ventured forward and settled her down and together faced the job at hand, birthing a child. A child that most probably has lost his father in this process, a beautiful boy child was born, it was such an amazing experience to be part of, this child came into the world loud and strong, that you could feel his purpose right there in your hands, every birth is like a miracle.

My first delivery and one I will never forget. Some moments stay gentle on your mind even though they were lifetimes away, you never forget the kindness of others or the good moments you enjoy, it is lovely that we get to keep them forever.

May love and kindness follow you all your lives, love is the reason we are here.

Harmon.

Jacinta

Hello I am JACINTA. I am an amazing tree here in HAWAII. We are all bursting with pride to speak with you, we felt your presence here and knew you were taking a break, and still we feel very proud you were here on our island. It's still like Wow! For us, we are so excited to be part of *the book*.

I am an elder here taking care of our young and helping them to learn the ways of love and patience.

Love we all understand but patience well! It is a learned practice, an art if you will, it's something we all struggle with from time to time. Impatience is the word you use to describe the opposite effect, very accurate indeed but it is never easy, as we want what we want, now! And that is not able to happen that easy as we need to take a lot of things in consideration first, sometimes it's a karmic thing but usually it goes back to law of attraction rules.

We need to be kind, we cannot be rude just because we aren't having a good day and in fact that's exactly correct, you are not having a good day because you are not kind to your self first, even you, like to enjoy the days as beautiful and tranquil as ever. Thoughtfulness to others is also a necessity, the more you give the more it returns to you ten fold.

Standing in judgement of others says a lot about you yourself, it says you're not personally happy with your life and that's why you can see others peoples flaws that reflect yours. When you understand these rules, your life will start to reflect the good things then everything you wish for appears in no time.

Understanding the law of attraction rules is a big bonus and enhances your life.

Patience is an incredible gift to give to yourself, usually learnt the hard way, once learnt never forgotten.

We value our lives immensely as every day is a gift, the sight of a new day dawning brings joy with hopes and dreams coming true. We love to keep our inner child ever present, as this is the best way to enjoy life, not getting to wrapped up in every piece of drama available. When you master patience, you will see the difference in yourself immediately, you will feel honoured that you are kind, thoughtful, and loving in every way. Then every amazing thing you ever wanted turns up in bucket loads, that's the law of attraction at it's best.

I would like to talk about eternity, we equate this, as a measure of time, meaning there is no time measure on it at all, as it will always be there ahead of us for always or forever as the saying goes. The word eternity means eternally yours.

We see you come into this world young and dependant on your parents and as you grow you learn to be strong and stand on your own, trying out everything that appeals to you. This is what life is all about, finding your feet and loving every minute you spend here on this EARTH as it is a blessing for you to enjoy each and every day.

I have a past life story I wish to share.

Many years back I was born into an Indian tribe, we were young and free and enjoyed growing up with all the freedom life has to offer, as we grew older we mixed with other Indian tribes but not before we fought each other perilously first and as the years advanced we saw the white settlers coming into our lands, that we joined forces to protect ourselves.

I was an Indian brave named WHITE CLOUD, later on I became chief of our respected tribe. As we grew I became very fond of RED DEER she was from another tribe in the mountains and daughter to the chief. We spent much time together although it was forbidden to marry out of your own circle. I wanted her so much that I sat in council with the chief to work out if it was possible, and as we did the soldiers attacked their campsite. We flew into action protecting the women and children first and then going after the soldiers, after they burnt the tepees to the ground, we chased them for miles and then returned to her people. The chief was so impressed he awarded me her hand in marriage. This was a great gesture as this cemented our relationship with both tribes. I returned to my family with my bride.

This life was an amazing one as true love is always worth the battle, we had children who were a mixture of both tribes and paved the way for others to marry. This started an amazing mixture of races and some still carry the genes right to this very day. I guess we were the way showers of that era. A life that stays with me to this very day, because love is what we come to experience and enjoy.

May love and kindness light your way.

Jacinta.

Alabasta

Hello I am ALABASTA.

I wish to speak tonight as I have beautiful thoughts to add to *the book*. I too am from The HAWAIIAN ISLANDS and in fact spent some time with you as the large fig tree opposite your hotel. I am one of many here and I span a large area and with all my branches anchoring back to the ground. I am hundreds of your years in age and feel even thousands of years of life still available to me, we are very strong trees with a great water supply due to the volcanic underground rivers that were formed many thousands of years before.

I have a purpose to achieve many things in this life, one is longevity as I too, represent the fallen trees in this area, which were removed for the many plantations that the land now grows the food the Island needs to survive on. We are here to help the humans as well but I feel mostly for the homeless, as we give them peace of mind and somewhere to rest that reminds them of the safety of home.

The animals and the birds also call us home. We facilitate everyone who needs us, we constantly see the tourists like yourself come and go here, looking at our beautiful branches and discovering the island, enjoying the parks, the beaches, and the old volcanoes.

We understand that we are on a spectacular Island in the Pacific Ocean and we also know and remember the time when our beautiful PEARL was attacked. Many of us still carry the battle scars of that era also.

War is horrible and it never helps anyone really, it is greed, hate, and jealously all rolled into one. We will never understand why this happens in the first place, invasion of another mans country is never an accepted practice, taking another persons liberty is a forbidden practice that should never happen at all.

We are all here to enjoy our lessons and we should be embracing our own list of lessons, not making it harder for everyone else. War has much to do with politics and monitory gain, and it is not a pretty thing. It takes generations to unravel the cost of war, never lone the loss of life itself. War breed's hatred and fear and leaves a horrible imprint on everyone involved.

This Island shares its grief and hopes they never have to face it again

Your soldiers lay within our waters, many never had a chance that fateful day, a full on attack, a surprise that was hard to endure, some of us still bear the sting of that day with iron pieces sprayed into us as well. Some of us were torn out by the force and their lives were over that day too. Bedlam is the best way to describe that fateful day.

If we relive that day we can still hear the screaming, the mayhem of everybody not knowing what to do, it was so sudden, buildings collapsing around us all. The bombers, the noise, the stricken people, everything in chaos it was worse than anyone's nightmare.

Even we do not like to remember that day.

We know life is short and everyday is a blessing. We also know this is not all there is to life, we come here to learn what it is our soul needs to encounter and choose the positive aspect of it.

The lesson is never wasted in anyway, every lesson is well learnt and recorded into our bank of memories in our very own AKASHI record.

Our AKASHI record keeps a track on every incarnation we have, however short or long, each time we incarnate there is always a reason for the life. It all adds up in the end and is a tribute to the charge we are following at the time, it gives us accolades to one day being able to master, a plan that will mean so much to us. A Master of evolution is achievable to most of us after a certain time. This is what we plan for, the greater good of the lessons and the incarnate time we spend here all add up for us to achieve great results.

My life is spectacular here at the moment, I resinate the good things and stay positive in every way, this is how we adjust so well to everything, attitude is essential, so to is love, sending love to someone who needs your blessings will also keep them in a positive state, which will also help you in return as it comes back to you ten fold.

Loving yourself is the greatest move anyone can make.

May I conclude the story of my life with a past life I loved.

Just as this life is beautiful, so too was my last, I often feel it in all its splendour.

I was a nobleman of much influence in the early days of VENICE ITALY. We created VENICE with its waterways and canals, we learnt to build homes higher and drier and made the canals the roadway so to speak. Much work went into the construction but it was very rewarding when it was finished, still to this day they sail the gondolas in the very canals we built and continue to build a better system for all.

In my time in office I met a gorgeous young woman who at the time intrigued me to no end. She came from a wealthy family but would not reserve her opinion, she was quite outspoken for that time and shamelessly would not back down. Her father was very distraught with her as she fought for a better life for women.

I was always quietly proud of her for having the backbone to fight for her rights. I was so smitten with her and asked her father for her hand in marriage. He was delighted and she agreed, but she had some terms and conditions to continue her work and I supported her in her role to teach the women of their true worth.

Together we travelled throughout our country teaching women how to be more proactive and respected. We also had children, and they travelled with us to show the world how a man and a woman with a family can unite the world. I believe we had an astounding life together, and many saw that a man can support his woman in her quest to change the past attitude and cultures that we're previously set in stone. It was time to unleash a new energy in that era. She was that energy and fearlessly fought the battle lines, day by day never giving in.

How, I loved her and admired her for the qualities she had, it was like, this was her personal quest, her special job to protect the female race, you couldn't but admire her as it came so naturally.

We lived a marvellous life together in the public eye but never once did we waver. We lived to love each other and help as many as we could, when I look back some days it was the fight of our lives, but it was thrilling and adventurous. I am sure I could not have enjoyed my life with out her and still miss her to this very day but I hold a precious thought that we would be together again some time in the future.

May you always be able to enjoy the love of your life, and live life to your greatest dream.

Kind regard's.

Alabasta.

Eldersklien

Hello I am ELDERSKLIEN. I am a splendid tree and part of a forest in northern NORWAY where we grow to enormous heights and we are strong and vital with life. We have been here for many centuries now and are still growing, we are fairly protected here, as we are very high up in the mountains, and we cope well with the cold conditions and thrive on love. We believe we are among the tallest on the planet at present.

You must forgive me as you caught me by surprise today as I was not channelled in to you at the first moment, but you called out to one to be spokestree on behalf of our forest and I was glad I was able to answer your call. I am the leader of the leader trees here and make the decisions on behalf of my clan. We have been here since time began on this planet and we are passing down to the next generations the joy of being alive and adding to the love this planet strives so hard to fulfil.

We have an immense feeling for life, as we give to ourselves first and then flow it on to all others in need, that is why when you go out to the woods or the forests you can feel the energy is different, calmer, quieter and so serene. This is because the energy around you becomes alive, and that is because we are so in touch with ourselves, our vibrations are electric to feel and stimulate those around us. This is how we communicate with each other, and we have the capacity to feel trees quite a long way away at times, and we can feel if it is urgent, so we can answer them as soon as we can.

We support each other completely as we are all one with each other and no one is greater than the other. We honour each other.

We are extremely large trees with a red bark exterior that keeps us warm during the winter months so we survive the cold. Even in summer here it is still cool by your standards, but we enjoy both seasons.

We also enjoy the sounds of birds and animals living their lives peacefully around us, looking after their young, and gathering food. We are grateful for the feeling of relaxation, and calm that comes over us as our auras touch each other and blend into the peaceful fancy of life. Gratitude is all that is needed for the feeling of being alive today. One has a sense of humbleness to be part of the universe, in all its splendour.

I say we, as I speak on behalf of all the trees here that we need to be heard and understood a lot more than we are now, however attitudes are changing and perhaps they will start thinking of us as a body with a heart and a soul just like any other living creature here, as up until now we have been mistaken for an object something to use as building equipment, medicines etc. We are indeed much more, we are alive with thoughts and a brain to think with and relate to each other through vibrations, which travel through the EARTH to each other in split seconds. We are a vital living group that should be admired. Our brain is not in one place as is yours but our memory is stored just the same as yours are in your mussels and in our case in the outer rings next to our skins or bark as you call it.

You are all amazed at the amount of rings you see when we are cut down, the rings you see on the trunks, they all mean things to us, some are our memory as we talked about before, we also store information that will be needed to help MOTHER

EARTH as she goes about her journey in the solar system. We also keep moisture so it is stored for leaner times and sometimes we have rings that protect us from the cold, layers, and layers of them in fact.

The rings you see are part of our body, then we have layers of light around us, which you call auras, we have many to keep us healthy and as we age these break down, actually the same as it is for the humans. We also have a time limit that applies to this life as we are not all meant to stay here forever as we have more important roles to finish where you call heaven and for us its called home, a place where we really belong, where our soul family resides and everyone awaits our return from this life that gives us a chance to learn our souls lessons, which we came to fulfil.

This adds to a resume of life and everything learned is never forgotten, it is revered and loved in detail.

Kept like a secret in our own AKASHI record, to be only of value to our selves.

I have felt very honoured today to give my details to add in what we call *the book*.

Safe journey to you in the unfolding of our lives, for all to read and hopefully understand us a lot more, so we can really be of assistance to mankind, to keep the balance on this EARTH in perfect shape for all of us to enjoy.

God speed and know our love follows your work and this book for the good of all mankind. Love and light be yours.

Eldersklien

Ondrayas

Today I call out to a beautiful soul tree that I witnessed being cut down in CHARLES STREET, TOWNSVILLE. My heart goes out to you and I have been talking to you through this whole process, hoping to be able to assist the soul return home gracefully and whole. You were an outstanding tree in size and many, years in age. It is sad that the humans cannot see the beauty in longevity, which would help us all, breathe a little easier.

He said my name is ONDRAYAS, and I welcome you and thank you for your words of wisdom that helped me tremendously this week. It surely was a trial to face one minute living happy ever after, and then the next people arrive and your whole life is taken from you in moments. I will spend a great deal of time healing my soul and recovering from the ordeal. I guess you always know time will be up one day but you never think it's today right now, that's the shock element to it. But here I am safely home with my loved ones who adore me, it's been a bitter and sweet ordeal, one that I will pray on for some time, until I feel the need to travel on and begin a new journey.

My life was an amazing mixture of love and light, one that I shared with everyone around me and I know I will be sorely missed, as I was the largest tree in that area, I stood in great stead with great pride and was the leader tree for that area.

Life will go on for all of us, but that doesn't mean we will forget the heartache that upheaval causes us, or the means by which they use to slaughter us, it is barbaric at best.

Another week has gone by since my return home and now I am feeling more grateful for the life I have lived while on MOTHER EARTH. The sorrow is waning and I am happier than ever to join in with my loved ones again. I have parents and sisters and a brother here. My parents joy to see me again was so beautiful, as they all wait our return home when we are away, as we go in and out of lives to accomplish our charges. A charge is a task given to us to complete certain things each life like love, patience, wisdom, and honour.

Our parents visit our light bodies that lay in state, awaiting the time our journeys take to fulfil our souls request, as they help us to complete our missions to assist in our masters degree to one day becoming A Master of Evolution, and after that we aim higher and start another degree that will take us many more lives of learning.

Life is ever lasting or eternal as you explain it.

We never give up we just try a little harder each time, that is also is a lesson for us.

I wish to talk about a program that we do, to be of help to each other to allow our wishes to come true or materialise in front of our very eyes, when we have a beautiful thought or wish that we cherish and are happy for it to succeed, we hold it in our hearts, keep it in our thoughts, visualise it being here and almost feel it is entirety, then it materialises quickly like it has always been there.

We are responsible for our requests and wishes, however if you doubt your request in anyway you then block it from coming through so, always keep your focus close at your heart level and rejoice at the marvel of the universe to deliver.

We call this the art of allowing.

I will spend quite some time here healing from this beautiful adventure of being a life giving tree on MOTHER EARTH, I do feel enchanted from the experience and in time I will move on to another challenge of greater ability.

I thank you for your kindness in helping me through this ordeal it meant the world to me to have you by my side, talking me through the process to keep my thoughts balanced and for now I will take a rest break and think of you fondly, kind regards.

Ondrayas.

Capricornia

Hello! I wish to answer your call as you ask us trees how we feel during those moments when nature throws horrific storms, cyclones and hurricanes around us and do we worry if we will survive.

Well actually the answer is no we do not worry, as we know life is everlasting, wherever we are, however there are times of great discomfort and lessons we need to face or learn this lifetime that are never easy but we too, soldier on or call our elders to help in a time of crises. They are always there to help us in a heartbeat to sooth our worries and talk us through all of our rough patches and this is how we learn to help others from our experiences, as we become elders in good time.

We understand the climatic conditions that play out here around us and we know we can be affected greatly. Certain weather conditions mix with each other to cause catastrophe events that sweep through causing havoc, there are reasons for these events to change situations, cleanse, and heal whole areas at a time.

Also changing weather patterns play an enormous role in these situations, as does karma. We never question why; it is as it is.

One could say we enjoy these times, it teaches us growth and to go with the flow.

We ride these turbulent times out high on energy and vibration, we feel on top of the world and if we break or loose a limb, we honour it and let it go. We don't allow ourselves to wallow or seek sympathy, our love for ourselves and gratitude for the life we live as a beautiful soul tree, here on MOTHER EARTH is enough, as we learn our soul lessons and complete our tasks.

Sometimes we are in awe of ourselves as we fulfil our journeys completely.

My name is CAPRICORNIA and I was indeed in the path of a cyclone as you call it, recently. I live on the east coast of Australia in tropical conditions and totally love my position here. We always succeed, as that is primarily our choice to love, guide and protect ourselves all our days.

Sending you love and light as you also follow your dreams to help others understand we are much more than timber at the end of the day, we are peaceful beings of light here to learn our life's lessons just the same as you are, we are all the same; we are you and you are us, one day we will all understand we are all one. NAMASTE.

Capricornia.

Simmona

Hello! I am SIMMONA. I have been waiting for a chance to connect with you for quite some time now. I am a free-living tree here in the AMAZON jungle. We are living the dream, we are enormous trees here to live our life and to help the environment. We all have important duties to perform some more than others, and the older we get the more output we can give as we grow. Then our capacity to develop our awareness grows and we become one with the creator on a personal level. We see and feel the direct vibration with the creator that allows us to feel and see and experience oneness as though we are just one being, one part here on this planet the other being in the space all around us, this is a magnificent thing to experience especially as we have our feet planted firmly in the ground.

Grounding, we hear you say that, staying grounded basically means keep your head in a firm place, do not give way to the whimsical cravings of life.

But you often say keep your feet on the ground and we smile as you don't always say what you mean but it is perfectly understood by you all.

Grounding to us is meant to connect us to the EARTH which brings in the peace, the love and the joy to our world which is a centre of calmness, when you feel this calmness you can connect to the centre of your being, which is your soul. Your soul then connects with the higher beings of light from where we come from. We are all higher beings of light here to experience this physical life in a form which helps us to understand the lessons we need to learn, loving, giving, helping others is where we start to learn.

You pick a form the same way we do, first we pick our bodies, our families, the place, and then the era which best helps us attain the best quality to live this life out. It is an amazing journey from start to finish and what we learn this life stays with us each cycle or life as it is known to you and is recorded in our very own Akashi record. Each life however long or short is beneficial to our existence in some way or another.

This method that we practise goes on and on for forever, just the same as your life does, whether or not we are currently in a physical body or at peace in our light bodies, these lives we choose are somewhat like a play game that we are learning to master, however while the humans are here in your physical form it feels so intense at times dealing with the physical strain of life, the never ending duties, the work load, the home life and care of others often take their toll.

We get ragged from the humdrum of life sometimes, as we learn and accept there are choices to be made. Every choice we make is a decision, so we choose wisely. We love our lives here in the jungle, in our natural environment along with all the other species as they too are living the dream of life.

Our thought process is similar to the animals and humans, but it is applied differently because we use feelings instead of words to transmit it through vibrations from one to another, so yes we can talk amongst ourselves when necessary. We are not talkers like you humans are but we can get our point across very accurately when needed.

We are all going through big changes at present as the energy is changing dramatically from fine tuning to a crystallyne appearance which will give us all longevity and help MOTHER EARTH stay on the right tract in the universe.

She is grateful for our help for with out each other, we would all have no choice or choices. We all live a life of peace and tranquillity and now we can enjoy interacting with the humans, something that others have only played with before now, and now we can write the words we wish to say with the help of our friend here.

It is amazing as we learn to find words that give meaning to what we wish to say, it will come easier with time as each of us learn this process, we share our abilities through our vibration and we all listen and learn and this is why when we speak with you, many of us have learnt the process already, we are very intellectual beings but we too come here with a clear slate so we have to learn from scratch just like you do.

We are enjoying the challenge and we hope the humans notice us and read the words that were so painfully selected in the beginning. We think now this has been an amazing journey for all of us. We look forward too many more words as we learn to express our opinions in the hope that we can all live gracefully together, always remembering we are all one; we are you and you are us. Our souls are exactly like yours. NAMASTE

Simmona.

Chessnett

Good Morning! A lot has been said lately on how we live and grow, but I have a point to make that I feel makes us feel special indeed. I am one of an amazing group, handed down in time that came here a long time ago, long before the lands had a name. Our tree ancestors grew at a time of the beginning of this planet, they too would not believe what we are doing with you at the moment. The veils are thinning and that makes it easier to communicate vibrationally with the humans at present, but it still takes a gifted person to feel us in all our splendour.

We were amazing in those days growing fast and filling the world with fresh oxygen, there were millions of us in all shapes and forms, and with nothing to stop us we had very long lives that lasted for centuries and spread our seeds far and wide. I still live in an uninhabitable jungle where our values are still appreciated to this very day, but I still know what is happening around us, above us and below us, as we know everything that happens. It is a very different world these days as technology takes over, we have lived other lives where we understand all languages and that is why it is happening here, it is a means to evolve.

We will live on giving and receiving love in everything we do to help this planet live to its full potential, we all have good reasons to want to stay a while as we are learning everything in the physical life to improve our souls purpose. The whole reason we are here is to enjoy each day that is given, and to teach us life is a transitory process and in time we return to our fold having learnt so much about this incarnation.

A physical life no matter what variety we choose to be, a human or a living plant enables us to learn the values around us of what our soul needs to learn, each day things crop up that teach us to grow and if we do not grow our lives become stagnant, and that lets in dis-ease which in time becomes disease of our fine bodies, if we do not try to move on and work things out, even if we do not get it right the main thing is we are not asleep in our life and we learn to take the good with the bad. If the bad or the hard stuff never came along we would never know the good when it arrives and that is what the lesson is, knowing life can always get better. Learning that life is abundant at all times and we are entitled to it. It is ours to reap however we choose so put your best foot forward and smile your way through life as often as you can.

We know you can do it, because we do, we do our very best to help ourselves and to help MOTHER EARTH each and every day. We live to fulfil our purpose to make the air you breathe and to sustain the energy on this earth. Every one of us, and that includes you have a purpose here to fulfil, we are all here at this moment to celebrate the changing of the light bands as we all become one with the universe. Our bodies are not that dissimilar to yours, given we look different in every way and ours suit the job we do and you get to move around a lot more, we have a body that suits our needs, but underneath we are the same souls. We all have individual needs and we balance each other, we are all brother/sister souls deep down here for the good of planet Earth as we learn the quests we came to conquer.

We all have missions to complete, sometimes it takes many of us just to hold the energy on our planet and this will last for many generations yet as the energy is changing and our DNA is becoming crystalline so we can last the distance in the solar system otherwise we will not survive, this will make our children strong enough to survive the changes.

Sometimes as souls, we do not see the big picture here while we are living out our lives. We are not aware of what we are developing for the future. We all have a big job to do while our lives go about our business learning our individual lessons as well.

We are all light beings creating a physical life here on this plane in this time space reality.

I am delighted beyond words to be able to assist in *the book* as we all wish we could write the stories of our lives to keep the memories precious and to be of use to another as we do record our own lives in our very own AKASHI records as these memories will be of value to guide us through the next lives we take. The next time we descend into a physical life on this planet or any other that we decide to participate in.

We know the enjoyment life brings and the value it brings to our souls. NAMASTE.

Chessnett.

Chathem Island Trees

Tonite I wish to contact a spokes tree on behalf of The CHATHEM Islands Trees.

I was asked to contact the Island trees from a young man who had harboured a secret, one which had a profound affect on him for many years.

This was their reply – The young boy would be one of many but he knows the laws of his people and the reprisals they talked about. We are sacred to the island, the people, and their culture, and indeed they would have been very strict about anyone visiting us on our Island. Stealing from us was an offence and carries a life time of regret, manifesting into different forms of hard luck, bad luck and sometimes depression, all of which is your own doing from the suggested mantra taught to the young at the time. We hold no malice towards anyone, this was a teaching, more likely a preaching. That was drummed into the young to show respect for themselves and the trees and anything else they wished to scare them with, let him know we accept the apology that he made to us, even though it was not necessary. NAMASTE

Chathem Island Trees.

Germaine

Hello! My name is GERMAINE and I am intrigued with *the book*, I too am interested in writing my life and times.

I am a very large tree centuries old and in good health, I believe I am in CAMBODIA where we are revered as ancient souls, which of course we are indeed. I work with the young trees to council them so they grow strong to withstand everything life throws at them and come out smiling, as they too one day will look after the young before them. We believe in looking after our own to facilitate strong ties in the future generations yet to come, if everyone taught that in the human world it would be a better place by now.

The one thing we see is the state of your health isn't as good as it could be, but rarely do you think of the generations that filter out from your genes, so if you use or misuse your body right now you are impeding the seeds you are sending forth to follow your family line. Damage to your genes is occurring at a great rate, much faster than you think, we see your children with syndromes caused by drug usage that could have been avoided. Everyone suffers, cancer rates are greater than ever, in adults and children alike.

There are disabilities galore, when will you realise everything you do is harming your children and this EARTH in total. War for one is the biggest disaster, maiming the young and the elderly. Wars still happen, there will come a day when we will all live as one in peace.

Life is a process and we are all working in the direction of love and kindness, slowly day by day we are winning the battle, it starts with you each and every day sending love and gratitude in every thing you do. Each one of us holds the power of our destiny right there in our hands. It's our destiny not anyone else's that is something we need to understand and accept. It is totally up to us, to celebrate this point and move towards it by accepting the experiences that come our way fully knowing this is what we need to learn this lifetime, good or bad as we label them knowing one can not live without the other. Choosing to accept each is as important as the other, if we didn't feel sad we wouldn't know glad or mad with happy and love with out fear.

Ancient souls are those that have travelled far and served many lifetimes, one after the other to back up the lessons that have been learnt and stored for future reference.

Ancient meaning the ones that came first and are still active today, the ones with great honour, great responsibility, and great love for the universe and themselves. We are all part of the great creator and his essence. The essence of life itself.

Germaine.

Caleb

Time will eventually fade our memories and allow a new life to emerge and now they relive the tales in talks, books, and movies for all to see and remember.

I myself have much longevity behind me and in front of me as we super seed into the next millennium and beyond. We all have an exciting part to play as we witness the changing of the light bands as our DNA changes to crystalline energy from the old carbon based cells which no longer represent us in these changing times. If we do not go with the flow we will not survive here on this planet, those who had no wish to change have returned home already before this process is finished. So that means the rest of us here are signed up for the ride, to help our Planet and ourselves proceed into the new position in the solar system.

So buckle up and enjoy the ride, it will take all our effort to rid ourselves of pent up old energy stored, like junk in our fine bodies, to clear ourselves of old patterns, old thoughts and out dated habits and changing our way to feel the love in every situation. Then and only then will we succeed and move forward. This will take a lot of work for us all to process, but we will win in the long run and our planet will be healthier and a happier place to be.

Now I would like to change the subject to politics, this is just crazy.

We see some who get voted in to represent the people and the country and then it doesn't take long until they cannot keep the promises they made as pressure gets put upon them to change their stance. This is not fair to the people who believed in them and the cause they defended. This is not setting a good example for anyone, one should especially, the chosen ones, be seen to be of good valour and consider honour a privilege to serve their nation or district as promised, as usually everyone feels let down afterwards, and we understand it isn't a easy task but one that shouldn't be taken lightly. We see them change their minds to fall in line to please the higher administration and not the people who voted them in.

Trust is then broken. Our lives depend on trust to deepen our awareness as we have much to accomplish in this life, it doesn't teach us anything if our elders disregard us, and we need them to set the examples to live by.

They will all learn this in time as they fail us and lose their positions they held so highly. Life is a learning kerb even for those who thought they knew it all.

Now I would like to talk about Love.

Love is a much better subject after all. Love is the most beautiful experience here on this planet.

Love is the reason we are all here, to see it, to feel it, to know it, and honour it well.

Love is like water, our fine bodies are largely made up of water.

Love is the same, we are love, we breathe love, and we give love and cannot live without it. Those who think love is underrated will learn the hard way as their bodies will decay just like it does from a lack of water, it will dehydrate and lose mental clarity. We need to love something, in order to stay on top of our game and loving yourself first is a great way to start, then love will flow in all other areas in your life. Loving a pet gives you unconditional love, like you have never known in your life and loving another gives us stability, balance and abundance in our lives. Receiving love is as good as giving it whether it is emotional or the physical touch each is as important as the other.

Living each day is what is the most important thing in all our lives, we are here to learn and experience the joy and the sorrow so we grow from every experience. This is why we came here to learn the difference. Life doesn't have to be hard; life is meant to be enjoyed.

Please know, we the trees love you very much, take time around us to ground yourself and breathe in the vibrations to soothe your tired souls. We are so happy to help you, love, and blessings to you all. NAMASTE

Calab

Cristo

Thank-you, I am indeed willing to share my life and times to add to *the book*.

We are very grateful to be able to translate to you to allow our life's story to travel on in time.

I am at this moment in time living a free life as a magnificent tree in the BAHAMAS, situated on the very north side, where it is a very pictures place, we feel very honoured to be here to give so much love and devotion to this area.

I am a star traveller who travels the solar system to live lives on any planet that fulfils my souls journey and destiny. We live out the lives that create the most beneficial outcome for us, so we can add to our honours list when we arrive home.

This new level takes us to a higher mark to achieve a charge that puts us in a better category the next time around, the one thing we strive for is to achieve a master in evolution in time after many lifetimes of loving and learning our souls request. We jump at the chance to return to a life that adds accolades to our already great resume, in the hope that it assists our plans to achieve our master's degree.

In this life we serve this great planet as she also responds to us giving us fertile ground and precious water to survive the seasons as they play out from winter to summer. We also watch and guide her into position as she does not have eyes to see with, she can only feel the vibrations given to her through the generosity of the crystal grids, the mountains, the trees and the rivers that run, and the ocean with its tide times, these are all factors that count to keep her on track and moving in the solar system. She has protocol to follow and without the help of everyone she would not succeed and survive, we are all very important in one way or another.

Past life

I once lived a life on this planet and my name is still remembered to this very day. I was known as the COUNT OF MONTE CRISTO, a little bit of a villain I am afraid, a mixture of good and bad trying to do good mostly but I still smile as I remember the life and times. They were hard days and a hard life to endure but the lessons served me well, where we mostly learnt from our mistakes to treat others as we would like to be treated.

Thank-you for allowing me to share my past life, sending love and respect for all you do now, for us.

Cristo.

Vincent

Good Evening my name is VINCENT. I am a tropical tree on the North West Coast of NEW CALEDONIA. I am very pleased to be able to tell my story so it can be written in the book for the rest of the world to see. I am also a very large tree of distinction and I am proud to represent the trees of this area. I too am a leader tree and hold many qualities to be of help to all the trees with any queries that might cause uneasiness in our form of life. We all value our journeys here as we are able to learn the lessons that our souls wish to understand this life, some lessons cause uneasiness at first then we agree to allow our teaches to proceed, dealing with the objective until we come to terms with it, then we are able to move on to higher ground with a much better understanding.

My name is VINCENT, a name of high standing in our family as it means strong one, one with poise and valour and understanding, and with love for all. I am situated on a high mountain overlooking a coastline, it is so serene and beautiful and I see all matter of things, the big ships sailing past, and people visiting our shore, usually for the first time on holidays (hol—e-days) as you put it, where they visit to enjoy the culture of the people and the Island itself. We are proud of our heritage as the people here have great respect for our lives and consider us an important part of the land.

I wish to talk about our futures, yours and ours and we are only here for short lives really when you think about it, most humans spend some time here between one and a hundred years and some of us can stay longer if we are left alone to do so. We all have things to work out and to learn different codes of conduct in our life times, this is something we get to keep for always, it travels with us each life time we have, only our physical bodies disappear so our souls are free to roam once again, to delight in a ethereal ascent back to our original loved ones, who await our return. This is the most exciting time for us to travel home after a stint here on EARTH with new knowledge and a keenness to embrace our souls journey. We are all grateful for the experience we have here.

I am known as a GALIDEAR (pronounced gal-i-dear) here, that is a tree that holds many distinctions of past lives both as human and as a living tree, having had many experiences to share with everyone and now that includes you as well, as we are now able to write our stories to share with your world. A GALIDEAR is very close to obtaining the masters degree and becoming a master of Evolution. Then I do not need to continue to fulfil these physical lives in order to succeed, I will be all obtaining, all knowing and all consoling, and can sit on the great panel with the valued ones that have represented us in the last millennium. It is such a great pleasure and an honour to achieve in this lifetime. I will be rejoicing and feel quietly proud of myself.

I wish to share a past life for you to enjoy.

I was a fishmonger, in my early days selling fresh fish to the people of our town, a job reserved for the very young. I was very good at my job and received a raise, that earned me a special place inside the factories and required me to visit the boats as they came in and I absolutely loved it.

I made a good living in those days for my family and changed the way we received fresh goods in general, keeping the fish cool at all times. This was a great breakthrough in those times and as a result the food kept fresher for longer. It modernised the whole set up and more fish could be bought in and we were able to reach out further a field, making it a global business, one that strived and is still in practise to this very day.

I continued to climb the ladder into management as the years went by, then I was appointed into the political arena where I excelled and had a great life and bought more modern ideas into being. It was a very rewarding experience, so worry not where you start out in life or where you end up, the key is to enjoy the journey in-between.

Much love
Vincent.

Regina

Hello! I am a strong upstanding tree of the river gum family situated on the MURRY RIVER in AUSTRALIA.

I am REGINA, I shine love on every one who visits, and they are amazed with this part of the land, next to the river.

I have seen many in my lifetime right back to the days of old when paddle steamers were the mode of transport. I have seen many people come and go as the tide of time fades. We tend to live many centuries in this one lifetime if we are left alone to finish our journeys. We do communicate with each other but not as frequently as the humans do.

We raise our vibrations greatly when we wish to communicate with our elders and piers and then we are able to get help, (you would call it counselling) it keeps us balanced and calm. We too worry at times when we fear removal or the like. Sometimes it happens and our journeys come to an abrupt end and we are sent hurdling home in a minutes notice. We too struggle and feel our soul is not ready for this event, however we have to come to terms with it as well. When we settle down we understand then, that it was part of our lesson this journey that we chose to return home in a hurry, teaching us life is not always perfect and that we should enjoy every day for the present that it is, as there are no promises of tomorrow.

Everything can change rapidly and it teaches us to go with the flow, we are always hopeful of all the tomorrows yet to come as we enjoy our lives immensely, however if our time is done we also rejoice in returning home where our loved ones wait for us, as these lives here seem like a long time, but actually they are but a moment in time in the scheme of things, as we are all eternal beings evolving our souls.

Each one of us is doing the same thing, growing our souls whether or not we are on this planet or another, we are all practising and learning soul growth. Many accolades are given to those of us who try to accomplish and even those who do not accomplish are rewarded and then given the chance to revisit it again some other time in the next few lives, it is not a requirement to push ourselves to the limit, quite the opposite really it is there for us to complete it when we are ready.

I wish now to talk about vitality, vitality is that special feeling, or (oomph) as you would say. I think it's not really a word but it describes it perfectly. Enthusiasm is probably the best way to describe it, a feeling of joy for something you do with all your heart, enjoying every minute of it. We feel the enthusiasm for life, our life, your life, our fine bodies of light that are a permanent fixture on this planet, which enables us to respond and look after Mother Earth so well. We feel the vitality of this life is a gift, a privilege to be a part of, seeing the vitality in your lives when you soar, at doing your personal best.

Your best is all anyone can give or ask for.

Until next we speak, love and light to you and those around you, may you enjoy all of your tomorrows yet to come, much love.

Regina.

The Leaning Tree
Mulgrady

Hello! I am so glad I am able to talk with you, they call me the leaning tree here in WESTON AUSTRALIA. I am aptly named I guess, because I have fallen due to the prevailing winds, that never give up, so it is easier to keep growing in that direction as going with the flow is easy compared to pushing against it, we don't see that as a reason to give up, just surrendering to life as best we can, living and loving our journeys to the end.

My personal name is MULGRADY. It is a classical name chosen with my family in mind, a family that is far from me now, my soul family in heaven. We can and do communicate when we wish too. I am somewhat of a star, people who come from all over the world, stop, and visit me as they travel by. It is so nice, and they express their views and talk about me, never dreaming I can understand every word as the communication with you has now educated all of us, to be more able to use our vibrations and feel, what it is, we wish to say in return. We are all very grateful as now, we can communicate on a better level, a level that gives us hope that one day, we will be able to all live together more peacefully.

I hope my story gives hope to anyone that has a disablement, a disability exists deeply in your mind first, because a disability is a strong growth lesson here in the physical life. You chose this to make you strong, it was the greatest thing you wished for, to master in this life and in doing so, you will be awarded great accolades on your return home, which will serve you towards a masters degree of your choice. Soul growth is the reason we are all here on this planet at this very moment, each life we accumulate growth that is so important to our overall outcome adding to our resume of life. It also is important to enjoy your life immensely and bring joy, love, and laughter into play each and every day.

I myself struggled in those early days with the prevailing winds, which really battered me around severely, but little by little I found a way to keep growing even though I was bent over and not able to straighten up at all.

I continued on growing and found my way growing along the ground, where I can also get nutrients from the soil faster than adsorbing it all by my roots. It shows you life can hand out harsh conditions and it makes you strive to find another way, there usually is another way around, it is like your saying there are many paths to the top of the mountain. Find your path and follow it.

The native people of this region call me WIRNDA NGADARA - The Leaning Tree. There are many of us who suffer from this infliction from the southerly winds, I am not the only one however, I am in a position where everyone can see me easily and I have gained notoriety in this position.

I am very grateful to be contacted and even more grateful to be mentioned in *the book*.

I wish to add a past life story of my own.

I was known as a missionary, many lives ago in the teaching of Christianity to the people of that time. We voyaged far and wide delivering the good news only to be shunned away, from society in general. Although we persevered and moved on many times, looking back now our work as forerunners of this planet, paid off handsomely. We did change opinions on a whole, although it was a lifelong dedication to a cause.

This was a great challenge of that era, but one we believed in wholeheartedly and as we look around today, it has opened up a new direction that we enjoy today with people being able to choose their own direction, one can choose to be spiritual and not be made to feel religious, as being spiritual is to believe what is in your heart and true to your soul. Our spiritual nature is to nurture our selves first and then pass it on lovingly, to be of service to others.

Thank you for taking the time with me today, love, and blessings be yours.

> *MULGRADY Known as*
> *THE LEANING TREE.*

MAGDALENE. *Our front cover tree*

I am very honoured to be chosen to tell my story in *the book*. I remember your visit here with us in the valley, you caused quite a stir that day, we were so surprised as we have many visitors daily and no one was expecting our greatest celebrity, to walk into our valley, and walk amongst us. We were so excited and grateful of your visit. Every one of us sent messages ahead of you while you walked the trail in STYX VALLEY, TASMANIA AUSTRALIA. Our spirits bowed to you that beautiful day, every forest you grace, dances and delights with enthusiasm, as you bring so much love and happiness with you, we are bursting with pride to spend a just a moment in time with you.

May we send our condolences on the loss of your husband, we have to say we knew he was ill with not a lot of time. You are a brave lady, to go through the changes life hands out. Moving on after an event such as this is never easy, and now a delightful new life ahead of you with a new partner and still continuing your work with us, we have to say we really appreciate it very much.

My name is MAGDALENE, a name of great importance, chosen to suite the spirit of who I am and who I once was, we always remember the great lives and now here I am having an extraordinary life once again with a different agenda, this time to be of service to the great MOTHER EARTH. I am a very large tree with great responsibilities to guide and protect our planet right into the next level of changes, which are always happening and will continue to do so, for a number of years yet. I am but one in a million, here to guide her, to stay balanced, connected, and in control of the alignment she is seeking, which keeps our planet safe for many years to come.

We are also important in the eco system here, to keep the balance in place for many more generations yet to come, to teach our young the way forward, to be strong to face what ever comes their way. We teach them to look forward and to never look back and to go with the flow and not allow difficulties to overtake them, to strive to go on no matter the burden or worry and to not give in and allow themselves to indulge in self pity, this does not serve anyone or any problem. Teach them they are in charge of their choices and better ones can be made and this will show them better skills to cope with all aspects of life, for the rest of their lives. Then you will see self sufficient young becoming valued members beyond their years, and ones you can be so proud of. Love and blessings

Magdalene.

Petrified WOOD known as YAMANTO

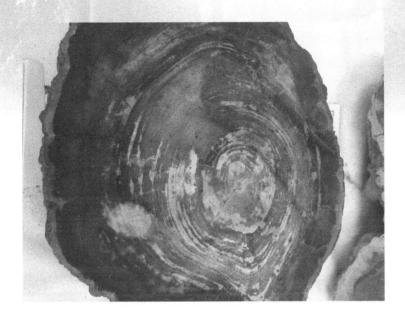

Hello! I met you two days ago when your hand was placed on me.

I was a beautiful living tree now turned to stone over many years and many layers of soil suppressed over me until I was discovered and dug out. I am but one part of a large trunk. I feel like I have been let out of the darkness and, feeling like I am alive again. I can recall the life I once lived.

Before now I have not been able to share my story with the rest of the world, thank-you for making it possible.

I am not required to address MOTHER EARTH as my time here as a living tree is done, however my memory still remembers the journey as the living tree. I have laid in the EARTH for perhaps millions of your years, until discovered some fifty years ago, since then my trunk has been cut into slices to display our magnificent patterns of life. It truly was a beautiful life living our potential to the fullest, enjoying each given day that came, flowing our seeds on to start new life wherever the winds blew them.

Our lives were perfect in the natural state where only the weather governed our path, wind, rain, and occasionally fire, were part of our daily lives. Fire ravaged through and left the dark colour embedded on us, and it also taught us to <u>respoon,</u> that is to respond to new growth in a hurry, by opening our seed pods to regrow to bring food to different species with our nectars and seeds. We all helped in the environment to nurture and feed the animal world, we were part of this great planet with our own protocol to follow as well, and we were part of a well-oiled ship with our own responsibilities to attend too.

I feel like it was an amazing life here in the wilderness, I don't recall the settlers as I was here during those early days when large creatures roamed around, it was a very natural life, the way it was supposed to be. I was an extremely large tree with great enthusiasm for life, at present my heart and soul is set in stone and I still feel reverence for this life, as there is still lessons to be learnt. I know I can withdraw my soul from here and return home at any given time I wish, but for now this earns me great accolades, which I choose to acknowledge and accept as markers on my evolutionary journey.

I believe your wish will come to you, that you will be given a piece of my trunk to cherish for all times, to be handed down, as a trophy if you like, to be a constant reminder of this time when we were first able to celebrate our words with you in what we call *the book*.

These words are our blessings to you, thank-you for being so thoughtful to read our words, which mean so much to us.

Love and blessings from YAMANTO.

Yamanto

Chamberland.

Hello! Sunshine I am so happy to communicate with you as you bring our news and the stories of our lives into the real world for all to read our words and hopefully from here we can learn to live together more peacefully and find contentment side by side.

We believe working together can make a huge difference on how we move forward from this day on. In the beginning of time there was great respect for each other and there was no need to create harm, as there is plenty of room for all of us, facilitating all our journeys in full.

I am at present a large tree, living my dream near a beautiful water source. I have grown very uniquely over a large number of years and have a great reputation here as a calm influence on all who visit, as we send love on to all every day. I hope our words reach many as we wish to be known world wide one day, so we can all celebrate a coming of age, a time when we can all understand the importance of each other, hopefully we can all be beautiful souls working together to build a life we will all treasure.

I wish to talk about togetherness, this works very well for us as we feel stronger when we can all share our lives in close contact, with each other and we know this works for the humans as well, feeling like you belong somewhere with someone is very comforting indeed. Togetherness is the wonderful feeling of being involved, deeply interacting with another person of your choice, free and wild, so your spirit soars and you are filled with delight.

I wish to talk about another subject, which is dear to my heart. I wish to address the need to talk about disfigurement or being disabled that makes you look different from others. This is a condition that is only skin deep, as underneath you are exactly the same as anyone else, however you are undergoing a transformation to your physical appearance to appear different to others for a cause. This cause is yours only and it is your calling to this life, a purpose if you will.

The purpose in this life is to shine and enjoy despite your difficulty to make the best you can in this life, sometimes it is caused by an accident that changes your pathway and you have to learn to change your life to accommodate, what you can now do.

There is often anger and resentment, to deal with first as your life changes and you have to learn to take on new challenges.

All of this is difficult at first, extremely excruciating to endure, however time heals all wounds and new pathways begin, it is something you never dreamed could happen to you, however it does and you have no option but to move forward and you are able to shine and feel the new purpose pumping in your veins, then you move with ease doing what it is you wished for, so long ago, before you came here and achieve the accolades that count towards your masters award in heaven.

Life often takes a strange turn or twist and it changes everything you know or believe in, even when this happens have faith that you and the universe are working together, working this out to suite your lifestyle to maximise the outcome in your favour.

I too am disfigured with everything that life has handed me from being trimmed time and time again and now a strangler vine is growing up and around my trunk and now into my limbs and branches, pulling me tighter and tighter, luckily I am strong and hope to outgrow this plant that often kills us out. It will be a battle between us, as this plant often uses us to support their own life, as they are not strong enough to support life by themselves. We strive to succeed and do the best we can always.

Love and blessings be yours.
Chamberland

Clementine

Hello. I am CLEMENTINE I remember your visit recently, taking your photos and talking to us, all three of us.

We too have much to say?

We live a very charmed life here in KURANDA in the ATHERTON TABLELANDS in AUSTRALIA.

The weather here is cool and the altitude keeps us moist and the rainfall is frequent.

We absolutely love our lives here and are happy to meet the visitors that come here every day.

We are humbled to be given the opportunity to be able to have our lives recorded in the book.

I myself am part of a threesome, the three of us have grown naturally together not far from the rainforest as we were once part of that forest ourselves, in the beginning before the road was cut in. We were so lucky to survive as so many didn't, now we live our lives in this natural environment loving every minute.

Our trunks appear to be tangled and as we grow more trunk develops into a pattern around the existing trunk giving an appearance of platting, which makes us look unique.

I wish to address the system where you choose which one of us lives and which ones don't.

I guess it comes down to your town planning they map out where roads and buildings go.

We are not disposable items, we come here to live our lives with love and respect for all but we do not get any respect in return. It takes us many years of growth to accomplish our lives. We will never be replaced again as each of us that goes can never be replaced as we are all unique souls with a mission to accomplish to save this EARTH from harm.

We protect from harmful rays of the sun on extremely hot days. We give MOTHER EARTH signals as to navigate her way through this solar system. There is so much more you do not understand, exactly what we do, or what we stand for.

We are so disappointed in what we see and in what we feel. We can't believe one person decides our fate and no one takes it upon them selves to help us so this is why we need to communicate with you now. It has taken a long time for us to find a way, we know some of you can do this but have been frightened to admit you could communicate with us for fear of reprisals.

We are very happy, time has changed enough for one clever soul to have enough grit to give us a voice. We are so thankful we have that now. There are many of us who want our side of life exposed so some of us need not die hopelessly, needlessly in vain because you can decide our fate. Sorry this is a rant in your words but we feel very strongly about getting our point through so, somebody needs to listen to us.

We know that in time writing in *the book* will help us, but not quickly enough, it doesn't occur to the humans what is at stake here, it is your lives here as well.

NO TREES – NO OXYGEN - NO LIFE ON THIS PLANET.

Do you really what to be the generation that wipes out life because of your greed and need for progress.

Some progress is great but please leave us here to enjoy our lives as we add so much splendour to our world. I would like to say to each and every one of you please think of us as you would yourself.

As we always say; we are you and you are us. Our souls are exactly the same as yours.

Much love and blessings and May GOD bless you all.

Clementine

Wilbour

Thank-you I do wish to engage you, I am very thankful of your time and energy. I call myself WILBOUR. It is a special name to me as it spans back to galaxy's of times past, different lives, different meanings. I am so delighted to be here and be important to those who are closest to me. I too have much love for the souls who care for me now.

We are very united with the force above where there is life there is love and salvation.

I am in the prime of my life with many more years of life yet to be of service to our great MOTHER EARTH to love and to honour her. I see many levels of existence, the physical one, which is the here and now, the present. Another I see is my future where I am going next time around and I see many jovial lives, which are consistently running at the same time, I feel these in all their glory. These lives are often known as past lives as all lives run on a parallel of time. We are enjoying all of them in different dimensions but each variation is as important as the other as we have much to learn.

Life is for learning so our souls can remember, that's the most important lesson here.

Our souls are not like clothes that are discarded often, our souls are the heart of who we are, and one that gathers information each lifetime as we learn responsibility and to create memories. Each life we have we keep our memories in tact.

I wish to talk about power, power comes in many forms like being a foreman, or a boss, a husband, a father or a friend, however never use power the wrong way, its lovely to be powerful with advice when someone is in need, but it is not right to use or abuse power to point out how to be above anyone else or this becomes ego based and egotistical in its nature. Always be kind whether you're helping anyone else out or not, no one likes a person abusing power or becoming self-righteous in any way.

We all wish to live a happy life and are blessed to do so.

We commend *the book* to deliver our stories as they are so precious to us and to date have never been shared before, our lives are not really that different, than yours. We see and feel much more with vibrations than most and now we are becoming apt in the art of words, it is breathtaking to us to be part of this special event, as one learns we all learn, that is the most amazing gift here. We are all here to love and enjoy our time on this planet at this given time. We are all souls from this universe marching time in these lives to learn how to function and love ourselves, and send love on to everyone else. These are all priceless lessons. We wish you all the greatest success in life, life brings something special to each and every one of us, with great achievements to fulfil.

Love and many blessings
Wilbour

Alsalvador

Hello! I am ALSALADOR. I live in the rain forest in CRYSTAL CREEK, PALUMA AUSTRALIA. This is an extraordinary place to live out your life. We live in bliss with a peaceful heart being nurtured with an abundance of water, fresh air, and all our family, and friends close by.

We adored your visit recently, we knew instantly who you were, there was such great activity amongst us as you arrived, we approve of your companion as he has us trees at heart, as much as he does for you. A new venture for him and he is rising to the occasion, we congratulate the both of you for taking the time to be with us.

We have come to love you very much. You are our rock so to speak.

I am very honoured to be chosen to give my story in *the book*, for everyone to read and to get to understand us better. We look different from each other but really we are not so different at all. We have a different disguise, meaning our bodies do not look the same as yours but our mentality, and souls still work the same, we are all here to seek a journey to fulfil our requests we designed for ourselves before we came, most will say no! no! no! Not me, I would have remembered that if I did. Well! If you are here, then I have news for you, you most certainly did. We all did, we have certain things to do and obtain in this life to give us the opportunities to qualify towards greater goals in our endeavour to achieve stardom in our eyes only, for that which we wish to achieve for a masters award on our arrival home.

It shows us here not to be afraid of returning, as this is what we repeatedly do, in and out of lives to learn the physical aspect that we cannot achieve while in heaven.

I am a leader tree like most of us are here, we are the older, wiser ones who help our young cope with all the trails, life hands out sometimes, mostly they do well but occasionally we have terrible storms, or cyclones as you call them and they can rip us apart in minutes, if we are in their pathway. These are the things they need our help for, just like you do as parents consoling a freighted child. Each of us young or older go through the same treatment and we lead by example, sometimes it is necessary to teach them to shed damaged branches, to cut off nutrients to that area, so it decays away so we can grow new branches and leaves, to start over and move on with our lives and eventually we succeed.

We need to be there to show them the way forward, then they become strong and full of knowledge, and in time replace us, as the cycle of life continues.

We are deep in the rainforest but we are aware of the planet we live on, we are aware of your lives also, the animals, and birds and fundamentally, how the whole eco system works. To some we may not look like we are intelligent but we have our fingers on the pulse, poised to act when necessary. We are wise beings of light with many years of experience under our belts, more than the average human at times, some of us have lived many hundreds and in some cases thousands of years here on this planet in the one lifetime.

We are peaceful, loving, and precious souls who come here to live our lives peacefully interacting, with everyone else to grow and to survive doing the very best we can.

We are so delighted to be able to have our lives made into words, as words are the best way to communicate with our beautiful soul friends at this particular time. The time will come when most of you will be able to communicate with us, with just one glance and we look forward to a time in evolution when we will all be one, one with each other because our souls are exactly the same as yours. Thank-you for taking the time to address us, we thank you. Namaste.

Alsalador.

Napaul

Hello! I am NAPAUL. I am so surprised to be talking to you this soon, as I only met you yesterday. I am an Elder here on this part of ROSS RIVER, as you can see I have had a particularly hard life especially with fires over the last decade with the weather slightly changing each year. We do understand the how's and the why's of this cycle as it is changing globally and we live with the road structures changing so frequently which cost us our lives so senselessly, this time the road changes have meant the water has been diverted once again, luckily we have long roots that can access water from the river, apart from that our lives are in a state of bliss.

My name NAPAUL, leads from a life many centuries ago, which made its mark in history.

I am so excited to be chosen to represent the trees in this area today. There was lots of excitement yesterday down by our river as you walked amongst us and took your photographs, you were very happy with your gentleman friend and we were so lucky to witness your joy.

As I said before I am an Elder that helps the tree souls in this area cope with all manor of stresses to sustain their lives bringing poise and dignity back to the forefront, teaching them not to worry about what they cannot change and to go with the flow with love abounding for the life they have in this present moment.

Helping them emotionally is a wonderful reward for our selves as well.

I wish to talk about manifesting, manifesting is an art given to every soul for the purpose of manifestation to bring requirements into the physical aspects of life.

Even the humans require articles to improve your quality of life, some assist and some decorate your lives, either way they are important for you to have the things you need to live this incarnation with ease. Everything from forks and knives to a roof over your head and everything in between, are things that assist you on your journey and can be brought in firstly by thought, then the desire to obtain it follows. We often ask and express our delight in having a particular thing, employment, a partner to love us, a child, a home, tools etc. It is granted in the spiritual world in seconds however than it has to materialise into physical reality.

In time given your behaviour toward this is genuine and you show kindness and love in everything you do it proceeds quickly but if you show no interest in it, it stops the flow and fails to arrive.

Some who practice this often, know how efficient this method is, everyone is joined in this process even if they do not realise it at the time, this is a given tool for this life, one of great importance.

As you come to understand it and how it works, it flows much easier and more things grace your life, with lightening speed, leaving you with the feeling you are invincible and incredibly loved by the universe.

Please share a past life with us that meant a great deal to you?

Thank-you I would love to, in a small corner of the world many moons or centuries ago in your terms, I was trekking the great mountains of my homeland, I was very good at this, as I had been raised nearby and learnt trekking was a great feat but we also learnt it could be fateful if not careful in certain circumstances. We became scouts, as we knew this area well, even in the coldest of winters. My friend and I became sort after, as we were very careful with the visitors who wished to go to the summit, it was not for the faint hearted or the ones with a dare devil attitude, it was only for those who had trained in endurance who could even think of doing something as great as this.

Generally it was a one time event, but for us it was our lives trekking the great mountains and learning every step of the way, no two days were ever alike because of the snow, we even learnt to hunt and survive in the harshest of conditions. We did this for many years until age prevented us, however we taught our young the joys of trekking and the art of survival in the harshest conditions known to man. A most enjoyable life to have lived and still after all this time remember so fondly.

Love and many blessings bestowed upon you.

Napaul.

Hollindale

Tonight I am speaking with a beautiful large fig tree in EUMUNDI, in QUEENSLAND AUSTRALIA.

Hello, I am indeed honoured to be chosen to write my story in what we call *the book*, we are a great attraction here it seems, as we constantly have visitors roaming amongst us on any given day, this is the life we chose to live here in the moment. We are many years in age now and have hundreds of years of healthy living yet to come, we are here for many century's to live out our dreams and desires and to procreate as much as possible, to teach our young, to learn to express our life's views, and to encourage others as well.

We have great purposes to fulfil, and GOD willing we will get to live out our beautiful lives here in peace and tranquillity.

We are star travellers from other origins having a resting life here with MOTHER EARTH at the helm, sustaining us to survive through this life, as we chose to be with her during this journey. We in turn get to help her for her kindness in guiding her through the celestial maize of the universe, and our intension is to be of service as her eyes to see and her ears to listen. This is indeed an honour for most of us.

I am an integral part of this community as I am a leader tree, one whose knowledge is invaluable to help others in need. I am strong and by far one of the oldest in this area.

We live by the stories told by the stars, we are in fact, all friends and old foes as we go in and out of lives over many millenniums, only resting for a short while in between as we all enjoy being on the job, learning to be of great value to the planetary alignment association, this is the area we chose to assist in as it is very interesting, and compelling to be part of.

My name is HOLLINDALE but my friends know me as HOLLEY. I too enjoy this life immensely as we are protected here in this spot and welcome everyone from all walks of life to visit us. They are so intrigued with our strong branches and valour, dignity or whatever you call it, that radiates resilience and strength. We also have powerful vibrations, which we use to protect ourselves with, and converse with our peers to communicate our messages of love and hope to each other.

I would like to talk about protection, their are different types of ways to protect yourself, for us we protect ourselves from violence by being non violent ourselves.

We protect ourselves from some insects that harm us buy releasing bacteria that is not acceptable to their environment or taste.

However sometimes they do quite a bit of damage to us first before we can activate our remedy to this situation, then we cast of all damaged foliage and new life takes its place, we are lucky like that. We love that we trees are becoming more valuable to the humans now and being looked on as partners in this life as we also provide you with gardens to sooth your souls and provide vegetation and forests that create the oxygen on this planet.

We are the Earth watches that keep an eye on everything that is happening, there are literally trillions of us going about our jobs all over the globe without hesitation and without judgement of how our human friends interact with us. We hope someday we will all be one with one another.

We love that you protect yourselves from harm as much as possible, this is your right to do so, and no one has the right to hurt or harm you because it suits him or her. Your right is to take care of yourself first after all, you are the most important person in your world, then looking after those that are close to you is vital, this then brings happiness and pride as an achievement in your life.

The one tool I wish to talk about is freedom, freedom to be who you truly are is the best learnt tool, sometimes this is clouded by the conditioning of family backgrounds, cultures and work places, but rise above this and show the world what you can accomplish anything you put your mind to by being your authentic self and not be driven by egotistical demands. This will be your greatest glory and bring joy to your life.

I wish to share a past life as you call it, even though all our lives run simultaneously at this very moment. We are capable of multitasking all our lives at the same time, that's why time travel is possible strait into other lives that are happening at the same time.

I have a life running where I am a Major in an armed force situation where the fighting is frantic one minute then it subsides for months at a time as the dissidents move on when battles become fierce. Then they regroup trying once again, to conquer what is not theirs to have, this is best described as an intergalactic war. One that will last for aeons to come as the rivals will eventually give up and move on, but in the mean time, we fight with all our might to hold our planet and the lives of our people here on our supreme planet.

I am capable of having this life which is a resting life for me and also knowing what else I take part in as well, however only evolved souls of thousands of lifetimes have this privilege and honour. I am indeed a very old soul by your standard.

I am most honoured to give my story to our chosen storyteller, to be shared in love to help everyone come to terms with the fact, we are all one. There are others that still do not understand as much as you do, you are fast becoming evolved humans, which we are so proud of and trust as our friends.

One day soon we will become one in heart and thoughts and live to respect each other. NAMASTE.

Hollindale

Telleado

Hello! I was so happy to meet you yesterday, it was my greatest pleasure to pose for your photographs. I am well known in this area as I have been here beside the train tracks in TULLY, NORTH QUEENSLAND AUSTRALIA for many of your generations. I see the trains taking the sugar to the market, and it is very interesting to watch, how your world works sometimes.

My name is TELLEADO. I have come from a far away place to participate in this life, to feel the joy of a resting life as a tree on this planet at this particular moment, so far I am loving my time here. I have grown with many layers of bark overlapping my main trunk, it gives us a decorative look and in time we grow into positive, beautiful beings of light that are blessed to be here at this very moment in time.

I am a leader tree here and my job is to look after our young and to encourage them to feel safe in the journey they chose to pursue at this particular time.

It is such an exciting time on planet EARTH at the moment, as she is shifting in the solar system so she can enjoy many more trillions of years ahead of her. This sift is a major one, as it is causing an impact on our EARTH in all areas, right down to our weather patterns, as it also affects our plant and animal kingdoms and yourselves as well.

We are all guided by the stars in the celestial patterns, as they guide us to deliver messages to MOTHER EARTH, to keep her on track. It also helps or hinders the humans at times, as it mirrors them to a degree, so they feel the pull of the universe in all aspects of their lives.

The best choice is stay calm and relaxed, as this way you do not hinder the progress around you, that was designed by you yourself in the life you have chosen to live this time around.

Law and attraction is my speciality, it is a very powerful choice in our lives, we use this in our everyday life even when we don't realise it but it is even more powerful if we use it with intension. Law of Attraction is a positive tool to use to create the life you really want, what you dreamed of and what you would love to participate in, will in fact come to you providing you do not stress or push against it, as it will only delay the activity longer, staying calm and being happy to wait until the universe delivers it to you personally, is so amazing. Life flows so make sure you go with the flow and not push against it, then life hands you everything you ever wished for, and it turns up in droves, which also makes you more positive, more sure of your self and love flows into your life in every way possible.

I have had many lives on other planets, that were busy lives of importance and responsibility just to name a few, this life is a resting life compared to those, here we grow and look forward to enjoying our roll here on the planet. Our wish is to send love and support to everyone and bless those who take the time to read our words for this is just the beginning in our plight to communicate with our beautiful friends, some of whom love and care for us very much, we want you to know how much we appreciate the time you give to us and look forward to a beautiful life together. I can easily say on behalf of all of us thank you from the bottom of our hearts. We love you all, Good day GLENDA.

Telleado.

Conclusion

My conclusion for book two is that I am so happy to be able to bring these messages through from our beautiful tree spirits. Personally I feel book two has more messages for us, as it is even easier to communicate with the trees, than ever before.

I feel it is a great honour and one I am very proud of. I am now travelling to meet the great trees on this planet and it is an amazing privilege in my journey to be able to assist them, bringing the life of the trees forward in their endeavour to be heard and understood.

I wish *the book,* the greatest success to bring their stories into the light so they can be heard and appreciated by all. I am hopeful that *the book,* will keep on circulating for many years to come, so everyone gets to understand the trees and hopefully we humans will learn to appreciate them knowing, we are all souls on our own evolutionary journey, and each deserves the right to experience our lives to our greatest expectations.

As they say love and blessings be yours.

Glenda Ungermann.

Thank You

I wish to thank my partner DON, for your wonderful love and support for helping me through every stage of book two, and sharing the delight and fun this book brings to our lives. Our moments with the trees are priceless memories to cherish for always.

Glenda Ungermann

Index

Y

CPSIA information can be obtained
at www.ICGtesting.com
Printed in the USA
BVHW070958210519
548903BV00001B/75/P

9 781796 001600